Dear Ed -

From a "Husker" to a "Tiger" - (1971 Alum)

Enjoy the Tiger-Husker Stories -

Thanks for all the F B + Memories.

Pete Roh

Mizzou Rah!
Memorable Moments in Missouri Tiger Football History

by Todd Donoho and Dan O'Brien

MizzouRah!

Memorable Moments in Missouri Tiger Football History

by

Todd Donoho

and

Dan O'Brien

Copyright © 2004 by Donoho Ink, L.L.C.

The trademarks on this product are the property of the University of Missouri and are used under a license from the University.

All rights reserved, including the right to reproduce this work in any form whatsoever without permission in writing from the publisher, except for brief passages in connection with a review.

For information write:

THE
DONNING COMPANY
PUBLISHERS
184 Business Park Drive, Suite 206
Virginia Beach, VA 23462

Ed Williams, Project Director
Steve Mull, General Manager
Scott Rule, Designer

ISBN 1-57864-284-1
Cataloging-in-Publication Data
Available upon request.

Printed in the United States of America
by Walsworth Publishing Company
Marceline, Missouri

For additional copies, log on to:
www.missourifootballmoments.com

MizzouRah!

Memorable Moments in Missouri Tiger Football History

by
Todd Donoho
and
Dan O'Brien

Foreword by Gary Pinkel
Afterword by John Kadlec

Mizzou Rah!

TABLE OF CONTENTS

Introduction - 6
by Todd Donoho

Foreword - 8
by Gary Pinkel

CHAPTERS

Uncle Don & Pitchin' Paul: Missouri 20, NYU 7 (Nov. 11, 1939) **10**
The Icemen Runneth: Missouri 45, Kansas 6 (Nov. 22, 1941) **14**
Mustangs Corralled: Missouri 20, SMU 14 (Oct. 9, 1948) **18**
Safety Last: Missouri 15, Kansas 13 (Dec. 1, 1956) **22**
Haas Cleaning: Missouri 20, Michigan 15 (Sept. 26, 1959) **26**
"We're Number One!" Missouri 41, Oklahoma 19 (Nov. 12, 1960) **30**
The One That Got Away: Kansas 23, Missouri 7 (Nov. 19, 1960) **34**
Orange Roughies: Missouri 21, Navy 14 (Orange Bowl - Jan. 2, 1961) **38**
"Oh, _____!!!" Nebraska 16, Missouri 14 (Oct. 30, 1965) **42**
Sugar Time: Missouri 20, Florida 18 (Sugar Bowl - Jan. 1, 1966) **46**
"Horsewhipped!" Missouri 35, Alabama 10 (Gator Bowl - Dec. 28, 1968) **50**
Brown Out: Missouri 19, Air Force 17 (Sept. 20, 1969) **54**
Staggering! Missouri 41, Kansas State 38 (Nov. 1, 1969) **58**
Tigers KO KU: Missouri 69, Kansas 21 (Nov. 22, 1969) **62**
Al's Well That Ends Well: Missouri 30, Notre Dame 26 (Oct. 21, 1972) **66**
The Butler Did It: Missouri 13, Nebraska 12 (Oct. 13, 1973) **70**
Turning the Tide: Missouri 20, Alabama 7 (Sept. 8, 1975) **74**
Standing-O: Oklahoma 28, Missouri 27 (Nov. 15, 1975) **78**
Trojans Fed to Tigers at Coliseum: Missouri 46, Southern Cal 25 (Sept. 11, 1976) **82**
Tiger Woods: Missouri 22, Ohio State 21 (Sept. 25, 1976) **86**
"Woods Has The Goods" Missouri 34, Nebraska 24 (Oct. 23, 1976) **90**
"M-I-Z! Z-O-U!" 1976 . . . . **94**
Powers Surge: Missouri 3, Notre Dame 0 (Sept. 9, 1978) **100**
Running Wild(er): Missouri 35, Nebraska 31 (Nov. 18, 1978) **104**
The Flea-FLICKER: BYU 21, Missouri 17 (Holiday Bowl - Dec. 23, 1983) **108**
Turnaround is Fair Play: Missouri 48, Kansas 0 (Nov. 22, 1986) **112**
Fifth Down: Colorado 33, Missouri 31 (Oct. 6, 1990) **116**
Stilled Hearts at Stillwater: Missouri 51, Oklahoma State 50 in 2 OTs (Oct. 25, 1997) **122**
The Flea-KICKER: Nebraska 45, Missouri 38 in OT (Nov. 8, 1997) **126**
Vindicated and Victorious: Missouri 41, Nebraska 24 (Oct. 11, 2003) **132**

Afterword - 140
by John Kadlec

Acknowledgements - 143

About the Authors - 144

Introduction
by Todd Donoho

October 13, 1973: Just six weeks after my mother had dropped me off at the University of Missouri, I sat down in my seat at Faurot Field with my dorm mates from Hudson Hall. We got ready to watch unbeaten Nebraska face unbeaten Missouri.

I was a freshman who came from a high school in Indiana and had little prior knowledge or appreciation of what Missouri football was all about. But that changed that glorious afternoon at Faurot Field.

I remember the sounds of Marching Mizzou.

I remember Herris Butler blocking a Nebraska field goal attempt.

I remember Tony Gillick's interception of a would-be game-winning two-point conversion for the Huskers that preserved the upset victory for the Tigers.

I remember running out on the field and leaping into the open arms of Tiger running back Ray Bybee. I leaped into a lifelong passion for Missouri football.

The University of Missouri gave me the two most important things that would shape my life, a Bachelor of Journalism degree and my wife of 25 years.

It also gave me some of the greatest memories of my life…various classes, professors, friends, parties, closing time at *Déjà Vu* and *Harpos*, and of course, football Saturdays.

Fast forward 30 years. October 11, 2003: My wife Paula and I traveled to Columbia from our home in California to visit our son Jeff, whom I dropped off as a freshman six weeks earlier, just as my mother had done to me three decades before. We planned our trip not only to see Jeff, but to see our college friends and the football game against Nebraska.

Well, Mizzou beat Nebraska that night, 41-24.

It had been 30 years between victories for Mizzou over Nebraska at Faurot Field.

I was a freshman in 1973, my son a freshman in 2003. And, as I had done 30 years earlier, Jeff stormed the field.

The game was over, but few left. We older fans celebrated in the stands while thousands of younger fans took to the field. The goalposts came down. We sang the fight song and clapped with "The Missouri Waltz." Grown men cried. I was one of them.

We Tiger fans have endured long losing streaks. We have been on the wrong end of some of the most infamous moments in college football history…a fifth down, a flea-kicker. It tests our loyalty, but we always seem to pass that test with flying colors. The bad moments make the good ones seem so great and so memorable.

This book is dedicated to the most loyal college football fans in America, the Missouri Tiger fans. Win or lose, we are Mizzou. We are Tigers. And at the end of the day, we'll all tramp, tramp, tramp around the columns with a cheer for Old Mizzou.

Foreword

By Gary Pinkel
Missouri Head Football Coach

When I walked off Faurot Field October 11, 2003 – through thousands of fans who celebrated our 41-24 victory over Nebraska with our players – I knew the impact this game would have on every Missouri fan and to our football program. That game, that win, was for a lot of people. When you go 25 years without beating somebody, and then finally beat them, it has a huge impact.

The Nebraska win was a defining moment for the direction in which we want our program to go. We have to win games like that at Missouri to achieve the goals we have set for ourselves. I think you can go to any program and look at a game or two that really changes the direction of that program. I would like to think the Nebraska win is going to be one of them for Missouri, and hopefully there's a few more down the road.

Before I got here, I studied the rich history of University of Missouri football. It has a remarkable history of winning bowl games and achieving great success.

Then there was a gap. There were reasons why the gap was there. I analyzed those reasons and put a plan into action. I am a process coach. I focus on the process. By doing this we will increase our chances for building a successful program.

My goals are much higher than upsets of Nebraska. I have a plan to make our program a national one that is respected around the country – meaning one that is consistently ranked in the Top 25 – preseason and postseason – and competes for championships.

I know I have a responsibility to all Mizzou fans to not only win at a high level – which we certainly intend to do – but to also have a program of great integrity, academic excellence and character development for our people.

I have very high expectations. We're headed in the right direction, but we're not there yet. We'll get there. And, with more wins for our program, we'll also create more memorable moments for our fans.

Gary Pinkel

Pitchin' Paul Christman (Missouri 1938-1940)

Missouri 20 New York Univ. 7

Uncle Don and Pitchin' Paul
NOVEMBER 11, 1939

The arrivals in Columbia of two future Hall of Famers catapulted Missouri's football team from conference doormat to contender. One game, more than any other, established Mizzou's national prominence.

When Don Faurot returned to his alma mater as head coach in 1935, Missouri didn't equate with job security. Mizzou had gone through 20 head football coaches in 44 years.

The rail-thin, lantern-jaw Faurot changed all that. In 1935 – the first of his 19 seasons at the helm – Faurot turned the winless 1934 Tigers into a respectable 3-3-3 squad. They improved to 6-2-1 the following season, finished second in the Big Six and beat rival Kansas for the first time since 1929.

The Tigers' national reputation didn't take shape, though, until Paul Christman entered the picture in 1938.

A multi-talented athlete, Christman originally hoped to follow his brother Mark into major league baseball. Paul did play baseball at Mizzou but his skills were much better suited for the gridiron.

Few, if any, could toss the pigskin like "Pitchin' Paul" Christman.

A Maplewood native, Christman quickly made a name for himself as the "Midwest's finest passer" during the 1938 season, his sophomore year.

Christman was already extending the scope of his fame in 1939 when he stepped into the New York City spotlight one mid-November afternoon. He emerged as one of college football's brightest stars.

Many of the country's most prominent sportswriters – including the legendary Grantland Rice – crammed the Yankee Stadium press box on November 11, 1939.

They were curious as to how upstart Missouri would fare against the 17th-ranked Violets of New York University. They also wanted to see for themselves if Pitchin' Paul Christman was as good as advertised – as good as Christman himself claimed.

The previous week, Christman had brashly predicted a victory over tenth-ranked and previously unbeaten Nebraska.

"I'll pass those guys crazy," he boasted. "I'll have them out of the stadium at the half."

True to his word, Christman passed for three touchdowns as Missouri jumped to a 20-6 halftime lead and went on to post a 27-13 victory – at the time Mizzou's most lopsided win over the Cornhuskers.

The Midwest writers weren't shy about praising the Mizzou star. One report noted Christman achieved success with apparent ease, claiming he performed "with all the nonchalance of a coed powdering her nose at the junior prom."

Christman seemed to approach NYU with the same cavalier attitude. The Violets could expect no shrinking violet.

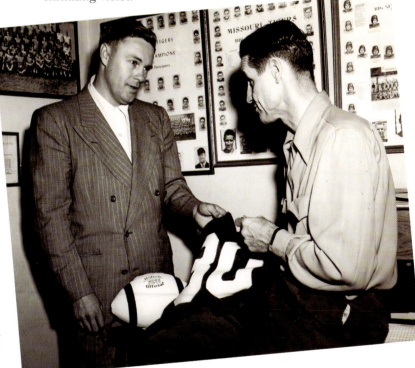
Coach Don Faurot centered his offense around his All-American quarterback.

Memorable Moments • 11

Christman with his future wife, Inez Potter, at Gaebler's Black and Gold Inn, a popular Missouri hangout.

"I'll blow those New Yorkers off the field," Christman quipped before the game.

And, like Joe Namath at Super Bowl III, Christman made good on his promise.

Even Babe Ruth might have been proud of Christman's one-man exhibition at Yankee Stadium. He clearly demonstrated to the 30,000 NYU fans – and the Eastern writing elite – that Pitchin' Paul was all he was cracked up to be.

More than a passing fancy, Christman had a hand in every Tiger touchdown in Mizzou's 20-7 victory. He personally outgained the entire NYU team and dominated both sides of the ball.

"The big kid from corn country stole the show," reported Arthur Daley of *The New York Times*. "He scored twice, pitched the other touchdown, called signals, intercepted passes, punted, tackled, blocked, and in general had a field day. This was a one-man show if there ever was one, a personal triumph for Christman, who did everything required of him and did it superbly."

Shirley Povich of *The Washington Post* was equally effusive: "The Dizzy Dean of the football field, young Christman did as he had promised to do. He came to New York touted as the Midwest's greatest passer, but he demonstrated that he could run that ball when he wasn't throwing it. They called him a 60-minute football player in Missouri and they were exaggerating only slightly. Against the Violet, he played 57 minutes."

His double duty at Yankee Stadium was typical Christman. During the 1939 season he played 417 of a possible 540 minutes.

The morning after the New York conquest more than 2,000 Missouri students (nearly 40 percent of the student body) waited in 16-degree weather to greet the Tigers' train as it rolled into Columbia. Christman, either unaffected by all the hoopla or

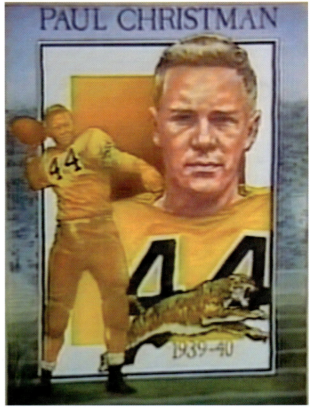

Paul Christman, All-American

(Below, left to right) Christman passes to Ron King, who makes a falling-down touchdown catch against NYU at Yankee Stadium. Notice the outfield wall.

simply worn out, slept through the reception.

"That snoozing is as characteristic of Christman as his precision forward passing," the *Associated Press* noted. "During the actual play he sparkles with the brilliance of champagne – in midweek practice he has all the fire and zip of stale beer."

The upset of NYU propelled Missouri to a 6-1 record and No. 12 *AP* ranking, the school's first ever Top 20 appearance.

The Tigers closed out the regular season at 8-1, won their first Big Six Conference championship and placed sixth in the final *AP* poll. They received an invitation to play in the Orange Bowl, another first in school history.

Christman established school passing records during his MU career (1938-40) that lasted for decades. The Tigers won 20 of 27 regular season games during the Christman era but no single contest did more to enhance the legend of Pitchin' Paul than his *tour de force* at Yankee Stadium.

A two-time All-American, Christman finished third in the 1939 Heisman Trophy balloting and fifth the following year. He is the only Missouri Tiger to place in the top five in the Heisman voting.

A Navy lieutenant in World War II, Christman played six seasons in the National Football League with the Chicago Cardinals and Green Bay Packers. He was the leader of the "Dream Backfield" for the Cardinals' 1947 NFL championship team.

Years later Christman became popular with a new generation of football fans for his colorful and candid commentary as a television football analyst.

Christman was a pioneer in the relatively new medium of television sports broadcasting.

Christman teamed with Curt Gowdy on NBC.

He teamed with Curt Gowdy on early telecasts of the fledgling American Football League. He joined Gowdy in the booth to call NBC's first nationally televised pro football game as well as the network's first Super Bowl telecast.

More than 30 years after Christman's Yankee Stadium heroics Povich continued to admire Paul – now for a different pitch.

"The running commentary brought to the show by Paul Christman was so superior as to expose as comparative dolts his opposite numbers on rival networks," Povich opined in a 1962 column.

Christman was a candidate to join ABC's first *Monday Night Football* announcing crew. But, he died of a heart attack on March 3, 1970.

Paul Christman was the first Missouri player inducted into the National Football Foundation Hall of Fame.

Christman did get his shot at major league baseball, a tryout with the Detroit Tigers (who else but the Tigers?). A power hitting first baseman, Pitchin' Paul allegedly failed to make the cut because his *arm* wasn't good enough.

Christman, flanked by fellow Missouri All-Americans Darold Jenkins (left) and Bob Steuber, upon his induction to the National Football Foundation Hall of Fame. All three were eventually elected to the Hall of Fame.

Don Faurot explains his innovative Split-T formation and the bottom two photos show the Split-T option at work.

Missouri 45   Kansas 6

The Iceman Runneth
NOVEMBER 22, 1941

Innovation produced devastation in one of the greatest seasons in Missouri football history. Just ask Kansas, victim of a 45-6 drubbing in the Tigers' regular season finale.

Heading into the 1941 season, Don Faurot had no quarterback to match the passing skills of graduated All-American Paul Christman. Who did?

Faurot's solution? A new offensive formation that proved more than a stopgap until another "Pitchin' Paul" sauntered forth.

Faurot's invention – The Split-T – not only revitalized the Missouri offense, but it also revolutionized college football. The Split-T is the granddaddy of all option offenses – everything from the Wishbone to the Veer.

Oklahoma coaching icon Bud Wilkinson believed Faurot's Split-T was "the most original and significant contribution to offensive football."

The formation draws its name from the wider splits by the offensive linemen, necessitating a wider spread by the defensive line.

In the Split-T offense the quarterback slides along the line of scrimmage, instead of turning from center to hand off the football. The quarterback reacts to the movement of the outermost defender. He either pitches the ball to a trailing halfback or keeps it himself, cutting to the inside. Faurot, captain of the Missouri basketball team in 1924, incorporated aspects of the 2-on-1 fast break in the new offense.

The plays were basic – a handoff to the "dive" man, a quarterback keeper, or a pitchout to the halfback. The results, though, could be astounding.

"With the quarterback sliding parallel to the line of scrimmage ready either to run with the ball or pitch out to a halfback," Faurot said during a coaching clinic in 1950, "you'll see more long runs from the Split-T than from any other formation."

Faurot's Split-T made an inauspicious debut. The Tigers employed the new formation sparingly in a 12-7 season-opening loss at Ohio State. But, they scored their only touchdown off the new formation, a 28-yard dash by halfback Maurice "Red" Wade.

"Not a hand was laid on the 'Tiger' sprinter as he ran straight for the goal line," reported the *Associated Press*.

Though not the real coming-out party for the Split-T, the game still represents a coaching landmark. The win was the first at the college level for Paul Brown, Ohio State's rookie head coach. Brown went on to a Hall of Fame coaching career in pro football.

The opening loss may have represented the proverbial calm before the storm. Once Mizzou got the hang of its new offense the opposition could barely hang with the Tigers.

Mizzou's "Touchdown Trio" of Harry "Slippery" Ice, Bob Steuber and Wade – running behind a line

Oklahoma Coach Bud Wilkinson called Don Faurot's Split-T option "the most original and significant contribution to offensive football."

Harry "Slippery" Ice

anchored by All-American center Darold Jenkins – bulldozed Missouri's next eight opponents by a combined scored of 219-25.

At season's end, the Tigers were the top rushing team in college football, averaging nearly 308 yards per game. Steuber was college football's third-leading ground gainer.

Mizzou's Split-T split the Kansas defense wide open in the regular season finale. Despite a downpour in Lawrence, the Tigers easily wrapped up the Big Six conference title and put a major damper on the Jayhawks' homecoming.

Six different Tiger players scored the seven Missouri touchdowns in the 45-6 romp. The Tigers wasted no time, scoring on a 49-yard running play just 90 seconds into the contest. Offensive tackle Bob Brenton carried the final 3 yards after taking a lateral from Ice for his first college touchdown.

Steuber and Ice were particularly lethal. The slippery one rushed for an astonishing 240 yards on only eight carries. Steuber raced for 158 yards on ten attempts.

Ice scored on a 57-yard touchdown run in the third quarter and set up a touchdown with another 46-yard gain. Wade carried the final 23 yards as he "crashed through tackle and into the end zone."

Steuber – a 6-2, 210-pounder with 9.7 100-yard dash speed – bolted for touchdown runs of 47 and 55 yards as Missouri outrushed Kansas, 449-69.

"Thrills created by the Tigers' terrible trio of Red Wade, Harry Ice and Bob Steuber sent more shivers through the spectators' spines than the frigid north wind which blew a

All-American Bob Steuber's school rushing records lasted for decades.

blizzard across the stadium," the *Associated Press* reported from Lawrence.

The margin of victory was the largest in the MU-KU series, which began in 1891. It remained the most lopsided score of the series until the Tigers throttled the Jayhawks, 69-21, in 1969.

Ice's 240 yards stood as Missouri's single game rushing record for 57 years. Devin West finally

Ice rushed for 240 yards on eight carries against Kansas in 1941.

"broke the Ice" when he rushed for 319 yards on 33 carries against Kansas in 1998.

While Tigers' offensive exploits grabbed most of the headlines during the 8-1 regular season, the defense was equally imposing.

Only two Missouri opponents scored in double digits. Missouri registered five shutouts, including four consecutive goose eggs to Nebraska, Michigan State, New York University and Oklahoma.

In 1942, Steuber – without Ice, Wade or Jenkins to assist – paced the Tigers to their second straight conference title, their third in four years. Steuber led the nation in scoring and finished as runner-up for the national rushing title. He topped all college ball carriers in average-gain-per-carry in both 1941 and 1942. Steuber finished his career with a remarkable 7.22 yards per carry.

Steuber was inducted into the National Football Foundation Hall of Fame in 1971. Darold Jenkins, a World War II bomber pilot who spent 17 months in a German POW camp, joined Steuber in the Hall of Fame in 1976.

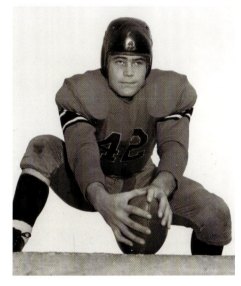

All-American center Darold Jenkins

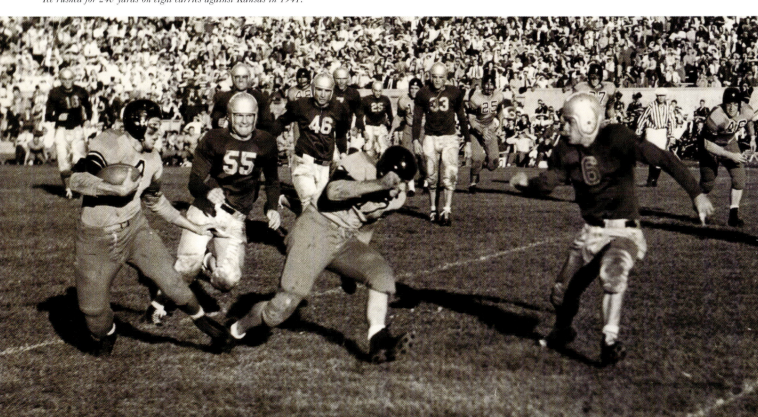

The 1948 official program cover

Missouri 20 SMU 14

Mustangs Corralled
OCTOBER 9, 1948

Missouri fans had the best of both worlds. They got to watch a marvelous performance by SMU's Doak Walker, one of the country's most gifted football players. Tiger fans still left Memorial Stadium with a victory, a landmark win. Mizzou's upset of fourth-ranked SMU re-established the Tigers as a national power.

The game was easily the most anticipated contest in Columbia since the pre-war days. The *Columbia Daily Tribune* warned Tiger fans not to lollygag:

"Columbia police and the highway patrol faced perhaps the toughest traffic in the city's history for the game and law enforcement officers and university officials alike renewed their last minute plea for fans to walk to the game—to start early."

Sage advice. A record crowd – 30,892 – jammed Memorial Stadium. Naturally, most were Tiger boosters, but SMU's special 16-car train transported a few hundred Mustang fans with the team.

Even Missouri fans were anxious to see Walker in action. Only a junior, Walker had already achieved legendary status. A do-everything player, Walker would go on to win the Heisman Trophy following the 1948 season. Doak Walker was the "All-American boy" in every sense.

"Oh, he was exceptional," said Harry Smith, a longtime Missouri assistant coach. "But there was nothing selfish about him. I talked to him after the game and he was a true gentleman."

Walker may have dazzled Tiger and Mustang fans alike with his one-man show in Columbia, but he had ample support. SMU quarterback Gil Johnson was one of the nation's most feared passers, while some Mustang fans wondered if sophomore back Kyle Rote could be the "the next Doak Walker."

The Mustangs scored 11 touchdowns in huge wins over Pittsburgh and Texas A&M to start the 1948 season. Walker scored four touchdowns and passed for three more in that pair of wins.

SMU, rated 13-point favorites over Missouri, carried a 15-game unbeaten streak into Columbia.

True to form, Walker put the Mustangs on top in the second quarter. His interception of a Tiger pass gave SMU possession. His diving, over-the-shoulder catch advanced the Mustangs to the Missouri 3-yard line. Walker scored two plays later on a 2-yard run and kicked the extra point for a 7-0 SMU lead.

Missouri threatened twice in the opening half, but the Tigers went to the locker room with a zero on their scoring ledger.

Quarterback "Bus" Entsminger ran the Missouri attack against SMU in 1948.

"It appeared that the Tigers might knock on the door all day without result," wrote Robert Morrison of the *St. Louis Post-Dispatch*, "but they found the route to an enhanced national prestige in a fighting second half."

With quarterback Guy "Bus" Entsminger at the helm of Don Faurot's Split-T offense, the Tigers churned out yardage and scored three touchdowns in the second half. Entsminger with running backs Mike Ghnouly, Dick Braznell, Nick Carras, John Glorioso and Lloyd Brinkman combined for 356 rushing yards on the day.

Entsminger guided the Tigers to a 70-yard drive following the second half kickoff with "Bus" driving the final 7 yards off tackle. Bob Dawson's extra point tied the score, 7-7.

Ghnouly's 34-yard punt return set up Mizzou's second touchdown, a 23-yard sweep by Braznell early in the fourth quarter. Dawson's kick gave the Tigers a 14-7 lead.

Later in the period Brinkman carried 40 yards to SMU's 6-yard line. Glorioso scored two plays later from the 2-yard line. This time Dawson missed the point-after. Missouri led, 20-7, with three minutes left in the game.

Walker needed only 50 seconds to respond. The Dallas native hauled in a long toss from Johnson at the Missouri 35 and streaked down the sideline to complete the 74-yard touchdown play. Walker's extra point cut Missouri's lead to 20-14 with 2:10 left to play.

SMU got the ball back with 1:20 remaining, but Brinkman's leaping interception erased the Mustangs' final threat.

A play late in the third quarter may be the most representative of the day. With the ball deep in Missouri territory, Entsminger found daylight through the Mustang defense. With Walker apparently blocked out of the play, the Mizzou QB appeared to have a clear path to the end zone. Walker fought through three Missouri blockers and further amazed the crowd, who witnessed the familiar No. 37 overtake Entsminger after a 57-yard gain.

"When I rolled over and saw 37, I had no idea how he could have ever made that tackle," Entsminger said.

The Tigers' drive stalled at the SMU 2-yard line, but Missouri had regained momentum and field position.

(Top to bottom) Entsminger breaks to daylight on the option; Missouri's Mel Sheehan (65) blocks SMU's Doak Walker (37); Walker catches Entsminger from behind.

(Right to left) SMU Heisman Trophy winner Doak Walker scored all of the Mustangs' points, including this 70-yard touchdown – but the Tigers still prevailed.

Missouri players congratulate Walker and his SMU teammates.

Missouri Coach Don Faurot was modest in victory and SMU's Matty Bell gracious in defeat.

"I never saw so many high-powered backs," Bell said. "That Entsminger was an All-American today. We were outplayed and outrun by one of the best running teams in the country."

Players from both squads remained on the field for nearly 20 minutes after the game to congratulate each other. The Tigers gathered around Walker for an opportunity to shake his hand.

"The whole team was outstanding," Faurot said. "This is one of my biggest football thrills."

His biggest thrill was yet to come.

Tiger players carry assistant coach Harry Smith off the field.

The 1956 homecoming program cover

Missouri 15 Kansas 13

Safety Last
DECEMBER 1, 1956

With former President Harry S. Truman in attendance, Don Faurot gave Kansas hell in his final game as Missouri's head football coach.

Faurot didn't necessarily save his *best* for last. But he always said his coaching finale at Missouri was his most exciting win, and undeniably one of the most dramatic victories and unusual finishes in the annals of college football.

The Tigers stunned the Jayhawks, 15-13, by scoring a safety on what was essentially the last play of the game before a full house at Memorial Stadium.

With 39 seconds remaining and the score knotted at 13-13, Tiger defensive tackle Chuck Mehrer nailed Kansas running back Bob Robinson in the end zone for the decisive two points.

More than 40 years later, Mehrer, one of 15 seniors on the team, remembered his surprise when the safety opportunity presented itself.

"Yeah, I was surprised," Mehrer recalled. "But I had a guy playing across from me who had sophomore written all over him. I hit him a couple times earlier and, all of a sudden, that time he wasn't there."

Though the play has sometimes been labeled a double reverse Mehrer says it was "just a little counter." Mehrer read it perfectly and, according to the *Columbia Daily Tribune*, he "slashed across the goal line to upend Robinson."

The wild finish wasn't quite finished. The Tigers returned the ensuing kickoff to the 50-yard line. A fight broke out, causing the ejection of the Tigers' Don Chadwick and the Jayhawks' Don Martin.

With 23 seconds left Tiger fans poured out of the stands and headed toward the north end zone. Missouri backup quarterback Ken "Stub" Clemensen ran out the clock as the goal posts began their descent.

The Missouri players carried Faurot off the field and straight to the dressing room where the retiring coach received a number of tributes, including a 50-foot scroll signed by the Missouri student body.

"I'll never forget it," Faurot said immediately after the thriller. "This one – because it was over Kansas, our kids kept firing away so

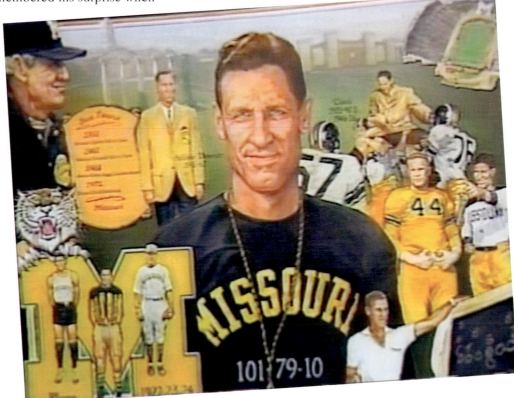

Don Faurot, the man who put Missouri football on the map

Chuck Mehrer saved the best for last.

determinedly, we won so dramatically, and the fact that it's so warming to go out a winner – was the most thrilling of my career."

The Tigers wouldn't say die. Playing most of the game without injured quarterback Jim Hunter, an All-Big Seven selection, they came back twice behind reserves Clemensen and Dave Doane.

Trailing, 13-7, late in the fourth quarter, Doane – seemingly trapped by KU's fourth down pressure – threaded a perfect 14-yard touchdown pass to end Larry Plumb through three Kansas defenders.

The jubilation died quickly, though. The Tigers missed the extra point after a bad snap from center. The game remained tied, 13-13, with 3:12 left to play.

The muffed point-after attempt merely set the stage for the thrilling climax. As the *Columbia Missourian's* Jim Creighton reported, the remainder of the game became "a frantic scramble for the lead."

The Jayhawks returned the ensuing kickoff to their own 25-yard line. After gaining seven yards on three plays, Kansas tried the first of two key gambles in the waning minutes. On fourth-and-three Kansas went for the first down. Missouri's Joe Wynn and Bill

(Below, left to right) Missouri defensive tackle Chuck Mehrer tackles the KU running back in the end zone for the winning safety in the closing seconds to give Missouri the victory in Don Faurot's final game.

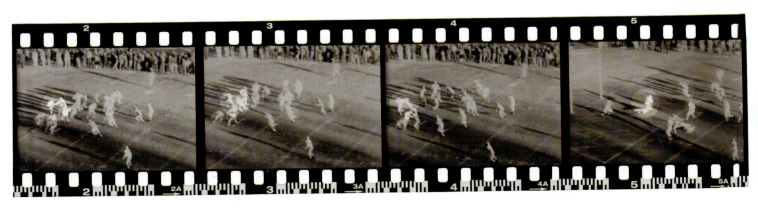

Don Faurot's last Missouri victory was his most thrilling.

McKinney stuffed Kansas fullback Homer Floyd at the line of scrimmage.

Clemensen took over as the Tigers' signal caller, but Kansas' double threat, quarterback/defensive back Wally Strauch, intercepted a pass in the end zone for a touchback. The Jayhawks took over on their own 20 with 1:24 left to play.

Strauch, who had thrown for the Jayhawks' two touchdowns, dropped back to pass and kept dropping until Missouri's Paul Browning and Bennie Alburtis dropped Strauch for a 16-yard loss at the Kansas 4-yard line.

Rather than run out the clock and settle for the tie, Kansas coach Chuck Mather gambled again.

Mehrer, playing his first game at left defensive tackle, quickly diagnosed the misdirection play and smothered Robinson for the safety.

"It was my fault," said a dejected Mather after the game. Kansas fans weren't inclined to argue.

The startling Missouri victory was Faurot's 101st in 19 years as the Tiger mentor. He closed out his coaching career with a 13-4-2 record against Kansas leaving the MU-KU series knotted at 29 victories apiece and seven ties.

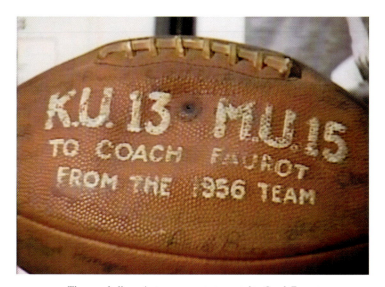

The game ball was just one memento presented to Coach Faurot after his final game as Mizzou's mentor.

Memorable Moments • 25

Bob Haas cruises campus with his college sweetheart, Judith Kaye Hutchison. They're still married.

Missouri 20   Michigan 15

Haas Cleaning
SEPTEMBER 26, 1959

Quarterbacks are known for their fourth quarter comebacks and last minute heroics. Missouri's Bob Haas, however, was an unlikely candidate to guide the Tigers to a miraculous win at Ann Arbor.

Haas, a backup quarterback pressed into service, sneaked across the Michigan goal line with just two seconds left to give the Tigers a 20-15 upset over the host Wolverines.

Despite his inexperience at quarterback, Haas guided Missouri to a 78-yard, 11-play scoring drive with less than three minutes to play.

The victory was especially pleasing to Dan Devine, Missouri's second-year head coach. Devine had learned to loathe the Wolverines during his five years as a Michigan State assistant.

"Our kids wore out, but they never quit," Devine stated proudly after the game.

Michigan had taken its first lead, 15-14, on John Halstead's 32-yard field goal with 2:49 left in the game.

"It looked for all the world like the Tigers had expended a noble but losing effort," wrote Rich Koster of the *Columbia Missourian*. "But then, dog-tired though they were, Devine's gutty crew rose up and for 11 plays were the 'greatest football team' Dan ever knew."

Missouri's chances seemed slim since starting quarterback Phil Snowden was ineligible to return to the contest due to the limited substitution rules of the time.

By his own admission, Haas wasn't the most potent passer to ever grace the gridiron. Still, he completed three passes during the Tigers' final march.

His first pass connected with end Danny LaRose for 12 yards to the Michigan 34.

After an incomplete pass, halfback Mel West took a handoff from Haas and picked up 11 more yards before the Wolverines knocked him out of bounds.

Haas passed again to LaRose, who stepped out of bounds after a gain of 5 yards.

A pair of incompletions followed.

On fourth-and-five from the Missouri 49, Haas dropped back to pass. Flushed out of the pocket, he scrambled 13 yards for a first down at the Michigan 38.

"Phil (Snowden) was the better quarterback but he wasn't a scrambler, strictly a dropback passer," said Norris Stevenson,

Back-up quarterback Haas was pressed into action for the final drive at Michigan.

a junior on the '59 squad. "Bobby was more athletic. I think it was just a matter of Bobby being able to scramble and move just long enough to get people open or where they needed to be."

With 1:10 remaining, Haas threaded a strike to end Donnie Smith between a pair of Michigan defenders, a 35-yard gain to the Michigan 3-yard line.

With the clock running and no timeouts remaining, the Tigers twice tried West on dives. The first picked up nearly 2 yards, but Michigan stuffed the second attempt for no gain.

With the time dwindling, this was it, do-or-die.

The Tigers could barely hear over the screaming Michigan partisans as they scrambled to the line. Haas took the snap and pushed through the Wolverine defense for the winning score – "push" being the operative word.

"Oh, I had some help," Haas recalled. "They had me stopped but Mel West ran up from behind and pushed me in. Mel and I had some laughs over that one over the years."

Wolverine fans weren't laughing.

Missouri had taken the early lead when West darted 46 yards for a first quarter touchdown. A 36-yard touchdown pass from Snowden to Dale Pidcock gave the Tigers a 14-6 lead in the fourth quarter.

Although Missouri led most of the way, Michigan had the advantage everywhere but the scoreboard. The Wolverines outperformed the Tigers in first downs (17-11), rushing yards (178-144), passing yards (134-105) and plays (74-54).

The Tigers kept the Wolverines at bay with four interceptions, including two thefts by Haas.

"I just happened to be in the right place for the interceptions," Haas said. "What I remember most, though, is making a number of tackles in that game. They had a big fullback, Tony Rio, who liked to just run over people. I hit him low and stopped him."

Haas also made a big stop on a Michigan 2-point conversion attempt. That prevented the Wolverines from tying the game, 14-14, midway through the fourth quarter.

Haas has lived in the Kansas City area most of his life, but business obligations necessitated a move to Michigan. There he attended a number of Wolverine home games in the very stadium where he performed his last minute heroics.

"I was able to replay that game many times while

(Right to left) Haas' pass to Donnie Smith set up his victory sneak.

I was there. It was quite thrilling," Haas said. "And, I got to rub it in a little when their fans started talking about the Maize and Blue."

Haas was a leader on the baseball field, too. He was elected captain of the Missouri baseball team his senior year. He was the Tigers' starting leftfielder in the championship game of the 1958 College World Series. His son, David, played in the College World Series for Wichita State and pitched in the majors for (who else?) the Tigers.

But, Dan Devine never had a better "relief pitcher" than Bob Haas on that autumn afternoon in Ann Arbor.

"You won the ball game for us," Devine told Haas. "That was the greatest clutch performance I've ever seen . . . the greatest."

The Tigers finished the 1959 regular season with a 6-4 record, a No. 18 ranking and received an invitation to the Orange Bowl – simply a prelude to the next decade.

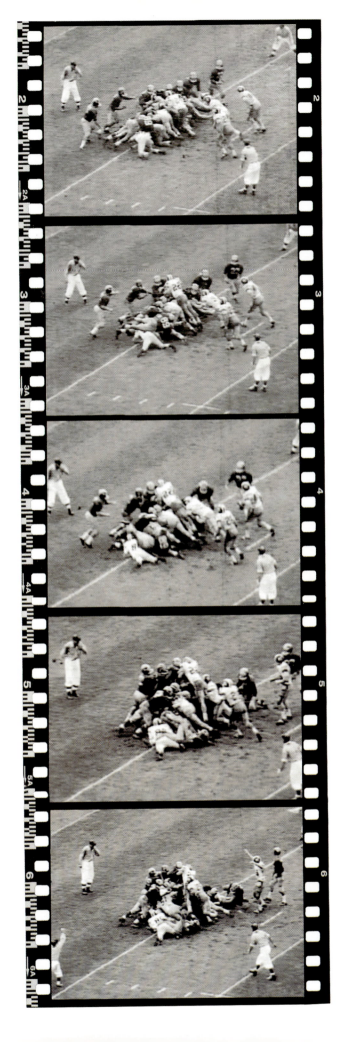

(Top to bottom) Haas sneaks in for the game-winning touchdown as his backfield mates give him a "helping hand."

Norris Stevenson had his greatest game at Oklahoma.

Missouri 41 — Oklahoma 19

"We're Number One!"
NOVEMBER 12, 1960

Missouri students proudly shouted it across campus. Columbia businesses answered their phones with it. The entire town, if not the whole state, was engulfed with the phrase:

"We're No. 1!"

In mid-November 1960 the University of Missouri football team – for the first time in school history – ascended to the top spot in both major wire service polls.

The Tigers, ranked second the two previous weeks, had thrashed Oklahoma in Norman, 41-19. That victory, coupled with a loss by top-ranked Minnesota, thoroughly convinced the pollsters.

Missouri received 34 first place votes in the *Associated Press* poll to seven for second-ranked Iowa and 22 first place nods from *United Press International* to five for runner-up Mississippi.

"They talk it in the streets, in the shops, at home, on the campus, in the town," wrote *Columbia Missourian* sportswriter Neil Amdur, "— well, just get a couple of Missouri people together and inevitably the first topic of conversation is: 'What do you think of those Tigers?'"

Athletic Director Don Faurot, who had coached some of the greatest Tiger teams of all time, wasn't shy in his praise of the 1960 edition.

"This is already the greatest Missouri football team in modern history," Faurot said. "They've done wonderful things for the school and the state."

Students, faculty members and townspeople turned out by the thousands to welcome home the Tigers after their long overdue win at Oklahoma. The Tigers hadn't won in Norman since 1936. They hadn't defeated Oklahoma *anywhere* since 1945. But that was only a preview for what was in store.

Mizzou fans everywhere awaited the next wire service polls with great anticipation. Early that week, both the *AP* and *UPI* gave Tiger fans the news they longed to hear: Missouri was No.1!

"The whole campus was buzzing," recalled Norris Stevenson, a senior back for the 1960 Tigers. "All of a sudden everybody knew you. We had more people at practice that week than most high schools have at their weekend games. The best way to describe it is that it piled on to the euphoria from that past Saturday at Oklahoma."

The No. 1 ranking was the culmination of a long but relatively steady climb. The Tigers began the season unranked but with a strong nucleus returning from the 6-5 Orange Bowl team of the previous season.

They opened the season with an impressive 20-0

(Right to left) Stevenson's touchdown run in the fourth quarter clinches Missouri's victory.

Missouri's victory was the first on Oklahoma's home field since 1936.

shutout of SMU and moved into the Top 20. They moved up gradually in the polls with a string of impressive victories over Oklahoma State (28-7), Penn State (21-8), Air Force (34-8), Kansas State (45-0), and Iowa State (35-8).

"Probably the most important thing and the reason we gelled is we had a real good senior class that had been together," said Ed Mehrer, a senior lineman on the 1960 team.

"We all liked each other, got along with each other and worked hard. And, there may have been a few overachievers."

After clobbering Nebraska, 28-0, for their seventh straight victory, the Tigers moved up to the No. 2 spot.

Despite a 16-6 win over Colorado and a loss by top-ranked Iowa the following Saturday, the Tigers remained in the second spot. Minnesota leapfrogged over Missouri into the top spot. Somehow, No. 2 wasn't good enough any more.

Oklahoma loomed next. Missouri wasn't alone in its frustration in the Sooners' "Snake Pit." The Sooners hadn't lost a conference game in Norman in 18 years.

"That wasn't one of Bud Wilkinson's best teams at Oklahoma; I think we kind of caught them in an off year," Stevenson remembered. "But, then again, you just didn't beat them down in Norman. We knew it would be a battle."

Stevenson believes the final score was not indicative of the fight in the Sooners. Oklahoma actually outrushed Missouri, 323-300. The Tiger defense had yielded only 72.9 yards per game in its previous eight victories.

Oklahoma even scored first, a 70-yard touchdown run by Mike McClellan on the fourth play of the game. Missouri responded with 24 consecutive points in the next ten minutes for a 24-6 lead.

The Sooners answered with another touchdown before the half and added another one late in the third quarter.

"It was 24-19 going into fourth quarter and we

AP College Football Poll
November 14, 1960
(First place votes)

	Points	Record
Missouri (34)	457	9-0
Iowa (7)	379	7-1
Mississippi (5)	362	8-0-1
Minnesota (1)	328	7-1
Washington	268	8-1
Duke	205	7-1
Arkansas	173	7-2
Navy	156	8-1
Auburn (1)	104	7-1
Ohio State	59	6-2

UPI College Football Poll
November 14, 1960
(First place votes)

	Points	Record
Missouri (22)	320	9-0
Mississippi (5)	284	8-0-1
Iowa (4)	270	7-1
Minnesota (2)	265	7-1
Washington	197	8-1
Duke (1)	120	7-1
Navy (1)	99	8-1
Arkansas	95	7-2
Ohio State	58	6-2
Auburn	54	7-1

Pollsters reward Tigers with their first-ever No. 1 ranking.

were thinking, 'Oh boy, we're into this one.'" Stevenson said. "We were able to do a lot of the things we were capable of doing but Oklahoma, that day, was playing out of its gourd. Wilkinson had 'em going – I think they used every trick play in the book. I think we just wore them down. Our backfield speed finally caught up with them."

On Missouri's first offensive play of the fourth quarter Stevenson dashed 60 yards down the left sideline – right past the Oklahoma bench – for a Tiger touchdown. Stevenson, who had scored on a 77-yard touchdown run in the first half, gave Missouri a 31-19 advantage. The Sooners never recovered.

Mizzou's Bill Tobin, perfect on five extra-point attempts, later kicked his second field goal of the game. Co-captain Donnie Smith, the Big Eight's leading scorer, rushed for his third touchdown of the game to give the Tigers their final margin of victory.

Stevenson finished with 169 yards on only 13 carries, his finest day in the Mizzou Black & Gold. At the time Stevenson's single game rushing total was the best against Oklahoma by any opponent. Dubbed by Dan Devine as "the best second-string back in the country," Stevenson was named to the *UPI* college backfield of the week.

That distinction didn't compare, though, to the team laurels the Tigers received a few days later.

"To be No. 1 – to be the best there is at anytime – even talking about it now kind of gives you chills," said Stevenson more than 40 years later.

The 1960 homecoming program cover

Missouri 7  Kansas 23

The One That Got Away
NOVEMBER 19, 1960

Who else but the hated Jayhawks of Kansas could shatter Missouri's dream season and send the Tigers to their most crushing defeat.

Though the NCAA and Big Eight later "officially" reversed the decision, Kansas' 23-7 victory ended the Tigers' place atop the national rankings and with it, their bid for a national championship.

The fervor for Mizzou football had continued to swell throughout the season as the Tigers racked up a school record nine consecutive wins. It reached a fever pitch following Mizzou's win at Oklahoma and the subsequent No. 1 ranking – the first in school history.

Tickets for the season finale at Memorial Stadium became prized commodities.

"The greatest influx of avid football fans since the invention of the pigskin will invade Columbia today and tomorrow for the nation's top football attraction—the Missouri-Kansas game," the *Columbia Missourian* reported.

For many a Tiger fan, a season-ending victory would be little more than a formality.

Head Coach Dan Devine knew better. Kansas, 6-2-1 on the season, was ranked 13th in the nation. Like Missouri, the Jayhawks featured a rugged defense and an All-Star backfield.

"A number of coaches say John Hadl, Curtis

Mel West (26), Norris Stevenson (40), Ron Taylor (12) and Ed Mehrer (35) keyed Mizzou's powerful running game in 1960 but the Jayhawks stopped the Tigers' sweep in this game.

(Right to left) The Tigers couldn't contain the Jayhawks' passing combo, John Hadl to Bert Coan.

McClinton and Bert Coan are the finest backs in the nation," Devine offered. "And I agree."

Devine was also worried about his own team, concerned the Tigers might be too distracted by the multitude of reporters and fans who crowded into Mizzou's practice sessions that week.

"Yeah, it was probably a distraction," remembered Ed Mehrer, a senior tri-captain. "There's also a thought that maybe we worked too hard. Coach Devine was concerned about a letdown and probably worked us too hard that week."

An overflow crowd of 43,000 – a Memorial Stadium record – watched the Tigers and Jayhawks slug it out to a scoreless first half. The Tigers nearly handed one to the Jayhawks.

In the second quarter, Mizzou fumbled on its own 11-yard line but held off KU with an impressive goal line stand.

The Tigers' offense couldn't respond. Kansas simply took away Missouri's sweep, the bread-and-butter of the Tiger offense. Mizzou's rushing offense, among the nation's best, produced only 61 yards.

"Give them credit," Mehrer said. "They figured out a way to stop the sweep and we couldn't get our offensive play call reoriented to run between the tackles. Once we did that, we started to move the ball."

Once the Tigers' offense woke up, though, it was too late. Mel West, the Big Eight's second-leading rusher, gained only 7 yards on five carries. Donnie Smith, the league's top scorer, picked up 14 yards on seven carries. Norris Stevenson, so brilliant the previous week against Oklahoma, rushed for only 12 yards on eight attempts.

"We were sleepwalking out there," Stevenson said. "We were still hanging on to the week before. The coach kept trying to get us prepared but it was just a whole lot to deal with. It was a circus going to practice and a circus coming from practice. You'd go to class and it was a circus."

The Jayhawks drew first blood. Hadl's 24-yard run off a double lateral set up a 46-yard field goal by Roger Hill early in the third quarter.

Hadl passed 19 yards to Coan later in the period for the game's first touchdown.

Coan set up the Jayhawks' next score with a 37-yard run to the Missouri 26. Coan's 2-yard plunge in the fourth quarter gave Kansas a 17-0 lead.

The Tigers finally came to life. West returned the ensuing kickoff 54 yards. He scored on a diving, 17-yard, fourth down pass from Ron Taylor.

But it was a simple case of too little, too late. Kansas tacked on one more touchdown for the 23-7 final.

"I think I did a poor job of coaching this past week," Devine said. "I recognized Wednesday that pressure was building up inside these boys. We tried to combat it by kidding around and saying this was just another ballgame. But it didn't relax them, did it?"

The third time proved to be a charm for the Jayhawks. The Mizzou game was their third of the season against the No. 1 team. The Jayhawks had lost previously to top-ranked Syracuse and Iowa. The upset also marked the third straight week college football's No. 1 team lost.

"I don't think I ever cried so much after a game in my life," said Norm Beal, a Tiger senior.

There was a silver lining in Mizzou's dark cloud. Kansas, the Big Eight champion, was already on NCAA probation for illegal recruitment of players, including Coan. With Kansas ineligible for post-season play, Missouri accepted an Orange Bowl invitation immediately after the game.

Two weeks later, the Big Eight dropped the bomb on KU. The conference ruled Coan was an ineligible player since October 26th, when the NCAA levied its penalties.

The Big Eight stripped the Jayhawks of their first conference title in 30 years and forced Kansas to forfeit the two games in which Coan "illegally" played – Colorado and Missouri. Kansas protested to no avail.

With the forfeit win, Missouri won the Big Eight championship and *officially* returned to unbeaten status.

"We're listed as undefeated but the guys know we lost it on the field," Stevenson said. "They played us and they won the game."

Beal readily concurs.

"They may have chalked up one in the win column but that is not a win to me," Beal said. "We lost the game on the field and, with it, the national championship."

The final wire service polls in 1960 – conducted *before* the college bowl games – awarded the national championship to 8-1 Minnesota.

Missouri dropped to fifth in the *Associated Press* writers' poll and fourth in the *UPI* coaches' poll.

Hopes of a national championship died on that November afternoon, but Beal and his Tiger teammates achieved a measure of retribution in January.

The Tiger defense holds Heisman Trophy winner Joe Bellino to four yards rushing.

Missouri 21   Navy 14

Orange Roughies
ORANGE BOWL - JANUARY 2, 1961

Neither a Heisman Trophy winner nor a newly elected U.S. President could prevent the Tigers from recording their first-ever bowl win. With President-elect John F. Kennedy – a former Navy lieutenant – among the 71,000 fans at Miami's Orange Bowl, the Missouri defense torpedoed Navy and Heisman Trophy winner Joe Bellino.

Missouri's 21-14 victory over the Midshipmen was Mizzou's first win in a bowl after seven previous post-season appearances.

The Tigers completely submarined the vaunted Naval attack, holding the Midshipmen to a net total of minus-8 yards rushing. Bellino rushed for only 4 yards on eight carries.

"I was sure we could stop Bellino," Missouri Head Coach Dan Devine told reporters after the game. "In fact, I was never surer of anything in my life. He's a great player but we have a great team."

The Tigers weren't so sure of success in the early going.

On their first offensive possession of the game, the Tigers drove to Navy's 1-yard line. The big play on the drive was a 43-yard scamper by halfback Donnie Smith after taking a lateral from fullback Ed Mehrer. That advanced Missouri to the Navy 9-yard line.

Another lateral turned into disaster three plays later. On third down inside the Navy 2-yard line, Tiger quarterback Ron Taylor handed off to Smith. With no daylight at the line of scrimmage, Smith tried to lateral back to Taylor. Instead, Navy defensive end Greg Mather picked off the toss and returned it 96 yards for a touchdown. Navy led, 6-0.

The Tigers nearly sank to deeper depths. They fumbled Bellino's ensuing onside kick. The Midshipmen then moved to the Missouri 20.

Senior Norm Beal, one of the tiniest Tigers, reversed Mizzou's fortunes. Navy quarterback Hal Spooner's next pass was intended for Midshipman flanker Ron Pritchard around the 10-yard line.

Missouri's 1961 Orange Bowl team

Instead, Beal stepped in, picked off Spooner's pass and outran his Navy pursuers – including Bellino – for a 90-yard touchdown.

The momentum – the entire game – shifted back to the Tigers. Beal, though, wasn't about to celebrate early.

"When I ran across the goal line I just had a feeling that damn thing was coming back," Beal remembered. "When you make a long run like that there's usually a clip or some kind of illegal block."

There were no flags. Missouri's blocking was not only legal; it was picture perfect.

"If you look at the picture, the blocking I had at the beginning of that return was just unbelievable," Beal said. "After that all I had to do was outrun Bellino."

Bill Tobin's extra point kick put the Tigers in front, 7-6, a lead they never relinquished.

"That (Beal's return) gave them the spark," Navy Head Coach Wayne Hardin said.

From that point Missouri's rushing success was a mirror image of Navy's futility.

Mizzou finished with 296 yards on the ground. Mel West rushed for a game-high 108 yards and Smith added 98 yards on the ground.

The Tigers marched 80 yards for their second touchdown, capped by Smith's 4-yard run early in the second quarter. Missouri led, 14-6, at halftime.

Missouri completely dominated the third quarter. The Tiger defense held Navy to only six offensive

(Left) Three weeks before his inauguration, President John F. Kennedy watched Missouri's Orange Bowl win over Navy.

(Below) Mel West has the Tigers on a roll.

plays in the period as Bellino rushed three times for a net gain of minus-4 yards.

"One of my biggest thrills of the Orange Bowl was knocking Bellino on his butt," Beal said. "He had this real low center of gravity and had big legs on him. They said nobody could go one-on-one with him but he got through the line and I got him."

Additional defensive stalwarts for Missouri included All-American Danny LaRose, Tommy Carpenter, Ed Blaine, Tom Hertz and Andy Russell.

A future Pro Bowler with the Pittsburgh Steelers, Russell ended Navy drives with a pair of second quarter interceptions.

The Tigers put together a 64-yard scoring march early in the fourth quarter. West was the big gun on that drive, but it was Taylor who logged the final yard for a 21-6 Missouri lead.

The Heisman winner finally got a chance to surface. Bellino scored the game's final touchdown on a 27-yard diving catch from Spooner. A 2-point conversion pass from Spooner to Jim Luper made it 21-14 with 6:56 left in the game.

Navy's final threat ended when Tiger Fred Brossart intercepted a Spooner pass at midfield as the gun sounded.

After Beal's return, though, the final outcome was never seriously in doubt.

"The final score is not indicative of the game," Tiger senior Norris Stevenson said. "We beat the stuffing out of those turkeys."

The Missouri players – this was pre-Gatorade days – tossed Mizzou's entire coaching staff into the showers, a first for Devine at Missouri.

The first bowl win in school history was also the first of four consecutive bowl victories under Devine.

The only bitter pill to swallow – the Tigers had no shot at the national championship. At the time, the wire services conducted their final season polls *before* the bowl games. Minnesota won the national title despite one regular season loss and a losing effort to Washington in the Rose Bowl.

"We probably would've won the national championship had they voted after the bowl games as they do today," Mehrer said. "Dan (Devine) always suggested that."

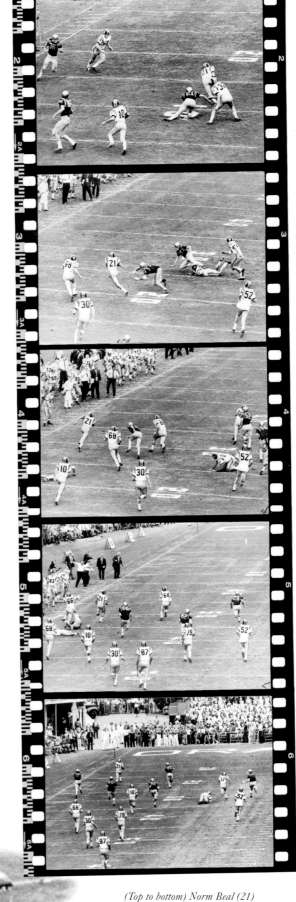

(Top to bottom) Norm Beal (21) turns the game around with this 90-yard interception return.

The 1965 homecoming program cover

Missouri 14   Nebraska 16

"Oh, _____!!!"
OCTOBER 30, 1965

A picture might be worth a thousand words but one word can be worth 15 yards.

One word not only cost Missouri 15 yards, but it may have also cost the Tigers a prime chance to upset highly ranked Nebraska.

For 54 minutes Missouri led the undefeated and third-ranked Cornhuskers before 58,000 homecoming fans in Columbia.

Down by two touchdowns early in the game, the Cornhuskers still trailed by a point, 14-13, midway through the fourth quarter.

On fourth-and-one from the Tigers' 35-yard line, Nebraska back Charley Winters drove forward for the first down.

After the play a Missouri defensive player – later identified as Tiger tri-captain Bruce Van Dyke – issued that "one impersonal profane word." An official threw his flag, assessed Missouri an unsportsmanlike conduct penalty and stepped off 15 yards to the Mizzou 17-yard line.

Four plays later Nebraska's Larry Wacholtz kicked a 26-yard field goal to give the Huskers a 16-14 advantage, their first lead of the game.

Missouri Head Coach Dan Devine was incredulous after the loss.

"I haven't had a satisfactory answer yet," Devine said. "But that call decided the game as much as any play on the field. The way I understand it one of our

Tiger captains (left to right): Carl Reese, Johnny Roland, and Bruce Van Dyke with Head Coach Dan Devine.

Missouri's "Mr. Everything," Johnny Roland

boys was disappointed because he hadn't made a tackle and made some comment to himself. Somebody must have interpreted the remark as directed at them."

The Tiger faithful, though hugely disappointed, still appreciated the valiant effort against one of the nation's powerhouses. Nebraska – ranked second in the coaches' poll and third by the writers – led the nation in scoring, rushing and total offense.

The 4-1-1 Tigers weren't exactly chopped feline. Led by running back Charlie Brown, Mizzou was the third-best rushing team in college football. And, the stingy Tiger defense allowed only eight points per game.

Still, the 6,500 Nebraska fans who made the trek to Columbia weren't quite prepared for Missouri's quick start. The Tigers jumped out to a 14-0 lead in the first ten minutes of the game, sparked by the running and throwing of quarterback Gary Lane as well as the power running of fullback Carl Reese.

Lane capped an 80-yard drive on the Tigers' first possession, rolling around right end for a 22-yard touchdown jaunt. For the first time that season, Bob Devaney's Huskers found themselves on the short end of the score.

After Tiger star Johnny Roland intercepted Nebraska quarterback Fred Duda, Reese scored on a 2-yard run. Bill Bates' second point-after kick gave Missouri a 14-0 lead, Nebraska's largest deficit since 1958.

Nebraska countered with a pair of second quarter touchdowns but Wacholtz missed one of the two point-after attempts. Missouri led, 14-13, at halftime.

The second half turned into a defensive skirmish. Midway through the fourth quarter Nebraska got the ball on the Cornhuskers' 40-yard line.

In seven plays they moved to the Missouri 35, setting up the fourth down run and the infamous expletive.

Devine wasn't informed of the nature of the penalty until after the game.

"I thought the head linesman had called a personal foul for piling on or something," Devine related afterward.

Big Eight Conference Commissioner Wayne

Duke conferred with the officials after the game and offered this explanation from the head linesman, Colonel Glenn Bowles:

"As the linesman marked forward progress of the ball on the Nebraska's first down play to the 32, a wrought up Missouri player voiced objection with one impersonal profane word. Colonel Bowles took exception and invoked the personal foul rule, which brought automatic 15-yard advance for the surging Cornhuskers."

Nearly 40 years later, Van Dyke gave his account:

"I was playing defensive tackle and the first time he (Winters) ran, I was very upset at where they spotted the ball. I might have said something then; I don't know. They ran the same play and I hit him with my shoulder but he slid over my shoulder and made the first down. So, again I was upset, I think more that I didn't get the guy, that I didn't nail him right at the line of scrimmage. I let out a cuss word very loud and the official threw the flag. The guy should have never called the penalty but it's just one of those things."

Van Dyke provided football fans many more glorious moments during and after his Missouri days. A three-year, two-way starter, Van Dyke was an All-Big Eight choice on both offense and defense. He played 11 seasons in the NFL and was twice selected to the Pro Bowl. His seven seasons with the Steelers' Black-and-Gold included one of the NFL's great memories. Van Dyke was on the field for Franco Harris' "Immaculate Reception" against Oakland in the 1972 playoffs. Van Dyke was enshrined in Missouri's Athletic Hall of Fame in January 2004.

Ironically, Missouri subsequently seemed to benefit more from the game than Nebraska.

"The Cornhuskers suffered what might prove an irreparable loss in prestige in narrowly escaping defeat against Missouri," *Washington Post* reporter Allison Danzig suggested.

On the strength of their "near miss" the Tigers moved into the Top Ten in the *Associated Press* poll. Nebraska maintained its *AP* ranking, but lost ground to Michigan State and Arkansas in total points.

The Tigers won their final three regular season games convincingly over Colorado, Oklahoma and Kansas and then knocked off Florida in the Sugar Bowl. Missouri placed sixth in the final *AP* poll, one spot below Nebraska.

Could Van Dyke's momentary indiscretion have provided Missouri's inspiration for its stretch run?

"Well, I'd like to think so now," Van Dyke chuckled. "But that's the first I've heard that suggested."

We'll never know how that lone penalty truly affected the outcome of the Nebraska game. As Devine suggested, under a different set of circumstances the Cornhuskers might have even scored a touchdown. But the audible indiscretion was the major topic of post-game discussion.

"It was a game of emotions but usually our kids swear less than any team I've seen," Devine said. "I'd probably have said something much worse."

You can *darn* well bet a number of Tiger fans did just that.

An All-Conference lineman for the Tigers, Bruce Van Dyke may have been misinterpreted by an official.

All-American tackle Francis Peay paved the way for a Missouri rushing attack which outgained Florida, 257 to minus-2.

Missouri 20  Florida 18

Sugar Time
SUGAR BOWL - JANUARY 1, 1966

Florida quarterback Steve Spurrier left New Orleans with every significant Sugar Bowl passing record and the game's Most Valuable Player award. Yeah, Spurrier had it all – all except a victory.

Missouri, leading 20-0 in the fourth quarter, withstood a furious rally by Spurrier and his Gator teammates. Spurrier smashed Sugar Bowl records for pass attempts and completions, passing yardage and total offense. But the Tigers stopped three 2-point conversion attempts by Florida to survive, 20-18.

Missouri's defense joined Florida in the record-breaking spree. Mizzou held the Gators to negative yardage on the ground.

The Tigers' pass defense wasn't quite as formidable but came through at the most critical moments. Tiger Jim Whitaker made the decisive play when he knocked down Spurrier's try for the tying 2-pointer with 2:13 left in the game.

"If we had just kicked the three extra points we would have won," Florida head coach Ray Graves lamented.

While the Tigers' run defense had little trouble wrestling the Gators, the Missouri backs ran wild. Charlie Brown, the Big Eight's leading rusher, enjoyed equal success against the Southeastern Conference foe. Brown, behind crushing blocks by tackles Francis Peay and Butch Allison, ran for a game-high 120 yards. Missouri outrushed Florida, 257 to minus-2.

Though the first quarter was scoreless, Missouri was clearly in control. The Tigers ran 28 offensive plays to only four for the Gators.

On the second play of the second quarter Brown took a pitchout from quarterback Gary Lane and followed Allison and Peay around the left side for a 10-yard touchdown run. Bill Bates' point-after gave Missouri a 7-0 lead, an unusual situation for the Gators, who had scored first in each of their ten games that season.

The Tigers quickly added to the lead. Mizzou's Ray Thorpe recovered a fumbled punt at Florida's 11-yard line.

On the next play, Mizzou's All-Everything Johnny Roland took a pitch from Lane, faked a sweep and then lofted a perfect touchdown pass to Earl Denny.

Bates nailed a 37-yard field goal just before the half for a 17-0 Mizzou lead. The Tigers' 17 points was a Sugar Bowl record for one quarter. The new mark wouldn't last long; Florida racked up 18 points in the fourth quarter.

Wary of Roland's punt return skills, Florida

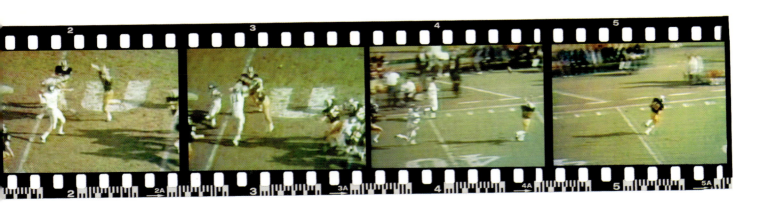

(Left to right) Gary Grossnickle (40) intercepts future Heisman Trophy winner Steve Spurrier of Florida, who struggled in the first half.

(Left to right) Johnny Roland (23) takes handoff from Gary Lane (16) and looks for Earl Denny (45). Roland lofts touchdown pass to Denny.

punted short throughout the evening. Missouri took possession at the Gator 49 on its first offensive set of the third quarter.

Lane's 25-yard run to the Florida 3-yard line put the Tigers on the threshold again. But, after a holding penalty, they settled for a field goal and a 20-0 lead.

The Tigers threatened again early in the fourth quarter. But, on fourth-and-one from the Florida 14, the Gator defense stopped the Tigers for no gain.

Florida's prospects seemed dim. Trailing 20-0 with less than a quarter to go, the Gators were starting from their own 14. Missouri's pass rush, which Graves called the best he'd seen all year, had stymied Spurrier through the first three quarters.

Spurrier, the future Heisman Trophy winner, was unfazed.

"He was like a crap shooter," Missouri defensive assistant Clay Cooper said. "When he got a hot hand, we couldn't stop him."

Spurrier ignited the crowd – 67,421 at Tulane Stadium. He completed six straight passes, culminating with a 22-yarder to halfback Jack Harper for a touchdown.

Graves then made the first of three similar decisions he would come to regret.

"When you are behind that far you need a shot in the arm," Graves said. "I thought a 2-pointer would give us a boost."

Instead, the Tigers administered the booster shot to Spurrier who "buckled under a heavy rush." Missouri led, 20-6, with 8:25 left in the game.

Missouri's celebration didn't last long. The Tigers fumbled at the Florida 10, a miscue which Spurrier converted into his own 2-yard touchdown run.

Roland, who admitted "he had us scared in the fourth quarter," batted away

Mizzou offensive tackle Butch Allison (70) paves the way for Charlie Brown (22), who rushed for 120 yards.

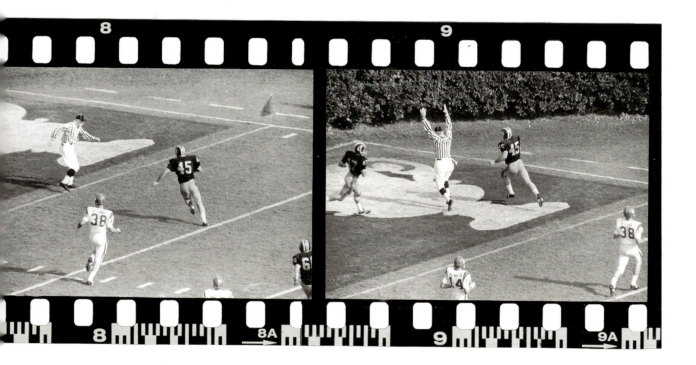

Spurrier's 2-point pass attempt. The Gators had cut the Tigers lead to eight points, 20-12, with 7:02 remaining. They also reduced their own point-after options.

After forcing Missouri to punt, Florida took over on its own 18.

Flushed from the pocket, Spurrier ran for 8 yards.

He passed to tight end Barry Brown for 15.

After two misfires, Spurrier connected with Harper, this time for 10.

Spurrier to Brown again for 20 yards.

Spurrier to Harper once more for 5 yards – second down at the Mizzou 29.

After a timeout Spurrier tossed a low one toward Brown. Missouri fans believed the Gator tight end trapped it (one official did call it incomplete), but the play stood for an 8-yard gain. Florida had a first down at Missouri's 21.

On second down, Spurrier lofted a pass deep in the end zone for All-American Charley Casey. Missouri's Gary Grossnickle and Casey leaped simultaneously. Grossnickle got a hand on the ball, but Casey made a sensational juggling reception.

With 2:10 left, the Gators didn't have much choice. They had to go for two.

Spurrier took the snap, rolled out and threw toward Brown in the same general vicinity as Casey's touchdown grab. Whitaker batted the ball away. No Gator could gobble up this one.

Florida got the ball back one more time. Spurrier completed three more passes but he and the Gators finally ran out of clock at their own 33-yard line.

Spurrier finished with 27 completions on 45 attempts for 352 yards, all Sugar Bowl records. Spurrier connected on 16 passes in the fourth quarter alone.

The Tigers' third straight bowl victory improved their record for the season to 8-2-1. Both wire services ranked Missouri sixth in their final polls.

"I told our players before the Nebraska game, 'if you play hard and up to your potential, you'll win,'" Devine said. "They played hard and up to their potential, but lost. They could have quit after that. I'm extremely proud of the way this team played those last three regular season games against Colorado, Oklahoma and Kansas and this one against Florida."

The Sugar Bowl was the final college game for 14 Tiger seniors. Johnny Roland, Francis Peay, Butch Allison, Gary Lane and Butch Van Dyke went on to pro football careers.

Missouri's locker room victory celebration was their third straight in bowl games.

The Tigers sacked Alabama quarterbacks 12 times.

Missouri 35   Alabama 10

"Horsewhipped!"
GATOR BOWL - DECEMBER 28, 1968

We were really horsewhipped.
We had a lousy defense.
We did not expect anyone to run down the field on us like they did, like they were playing a barber college.
They toyed with us like children.

These were the words of Alabama Coach Paul "Bear" Bryant after the 1968 Gator Bowl against Missouri — a game in which the Tigers thoroughly crushed the Crimson Tide, 35-10.

Bryant sang a different tune before the game. He told reporters this was his best defensive team ever, a team that had made great strides late in the season to finish with five wins in a row.

"We've got quite a football team now...you'd better believe it," said a confident Bryant.

He had good reason to feel that way. The Crimson Tide lost only two games during the season by a total of three points. For added incentive, if 12th ranked Alabama were to beat Missouri in the Gator Bowl, it would virtually ensure the Crimson Tide their 10th straight season ranked in the Top Ten.

Contrast streaking Alabama with slumping Missouri. The Tigers were 7-and-3 but lost their final two games of the regular season. No one was sure how Mizzou would play against the Tide until the week before the game. But, Missouri Coach Dan Devine told reporters his team had a tremendous week of practice, perhaps its best ever.

"We've never had a team more ready for a game. We clinched it earlier in the week," he said.

Any doubts the Tigers were prepared for the game were quickly erased on the first play from scrimmage. Quarterback Terry McMillan took off around right end and pitched the ball to running back

Missouri's Dan Devine and Alabama's Paul "Bear" Bryant prior to the first-ever matchup between the Tigers and Crimson Tide.

Memorable Moments • 51

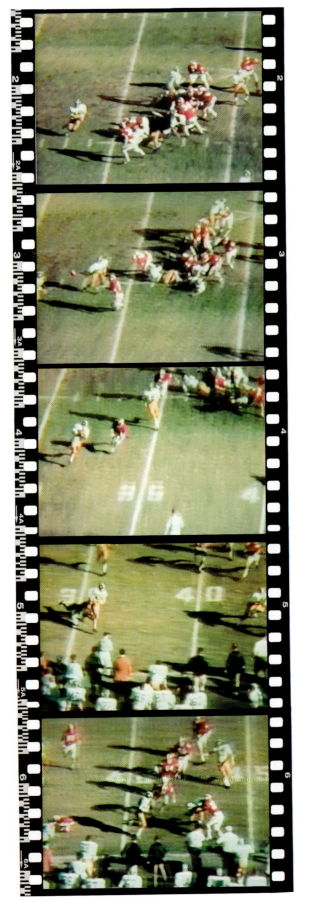

(Top to bottom) Tigers run the option to perfection. Terry McMillan (18) pitches to Greg Cook (25), who rushed for 179 yards against Alabama.

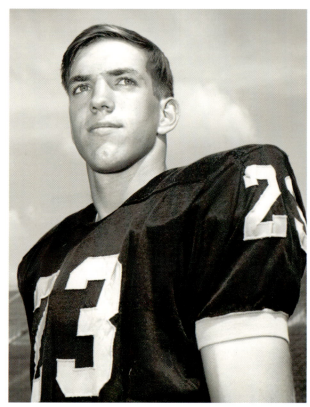

All-American Roger Wehrli honeymooned at the Gator Bowl and made a key interception.

Greg Cook. Cook left a wave of Tide defenders in his wake for a 33-yard gain. Down the field the Tigers drove with McMillan working the option to perfection, either keeping the ball, or pitching it to Cook. After 11 plays, McMillan scored on a 4-yard run to give the Tigers a 7-0 lead.

The Tigers running attack and staunch defense dominated the first quarter, yet they only had one score to show for their efforts.

McMillan attempted only six passes on the day. Alabama's Donnie Sutton intercepted one and returned it 38 yards for a touchdown. Game tied 7-7.

From that point on, Devine and company chose to keep the ball on the ground, and from that point on Missouri was a runaway locomotive.

The score may not have shown the Tigers' dominance until the fourth quarter when Mizzou blew the game open with three touchdowns. The Tigers rushed for 402 yards with Cook accounting for 179 yards on 27 carries. He also scored on a 37-yard run. McMillan ran for 76 yards and three touchdowns.

How potent was the Missouri rushing attack? The Tigers did not complete a single pass. They didn't have to. McMillan was 0-for-6 with two interceptions, yet he was the game's most valuable player. How many quarterbacks have won a game

MVP award with zero yards passing? That's how dominant Mizzou's rushing game was. And what made the Missouri effort even more remarkable was that this performance was against an Alabama defense, which gave up an average of only 85 yards a game on the ground during the season.

But, there's another side to this Tiger victory — the defense. While Bryant was bragging about his defense before the game, Missouri's defense did its talking during the game. The Tiger defense held Alabama to just six first downs. Alabama had a mere 32 yards in total offense.

The most impressive stat for Mizzou — the Tiger defenders sacked the Tide quarterbacks an amazing 12 times, and when they were able to get the ball off, Alabama's signal callers suffered crucial interceptions. Dennis Poppe returned one interception 47 yards for a touchdown, and newlywed Roger Wehrli (one of four Tiger players on their honeymoons in Florida that week) returned an interception 21 yards to the Alabama 21-yard line. That set up the first of three Missouri fourth quarter touchdowns to put the game out of reach.

The game wasn't as close as the 35-10 score. It could have been worse for Alabama. Wehrli had a 60-yard punt return for a touchdown called back because of a penalty. All of this was not lost on coach Bryant.

"They beat us every way known to man. They out-everythinged us. We were really fortunate. The Tigers deserved to beat us by more points than they did," Bryant told reporters after the game. "Of course, it was like any other college football game. The difference was in the preparation and coaching and there was a lot of difference today."

Bryant may have lost the game, but he did not lose his sense of humor:

"We would have been better off if my game plan had

Terry McMillan (18) scored three touchdowns.

called for a quarterback sneak on every play with, now and then, a quick kick thrown in."

Missouri's Dan Devine wasn't about to pour it on Alabama in post-game interviews:

"The fact that we beat him (Bryant) doesn't make the victory any better. He took the time to walk over to our hotel and meet my wife and kids last night. In fact, we're proud and humble that we could beat a Bryant-coached Alabama team."

The 25-point loss was Bryant's worst defeat at that time in his 11-year career at Alabama. The loss also ended Alabama's nine-year streak of finishing in the *Associated Press* Top Ten. Instead, it was the Tigers that climbed in the rankings, finishing ninth in the *Associated Press* Poll. The victory also set the stage for Mizzou's 1969 season, arguably the most exciting football season in Missouri history.

Quarterback McMillan was the Gator Bowl MVP despite zero yards passing.

Missouri Coach Dan Devine is head and shoulders above the rest.

The 1969 Missouri vs. Air Force program cover

Missouri 19   Air Force 17

Brown Out

SEPTEMBER 20, 1969

Air Force had the game socked away. The Falcons had it! They had just pulled out a miraculous come-from-behind win over Missouri in the closing seconds – or so it seemed.

But Mizzou had its own miracle workers. Certainly, Tiger fans looked to quarterback Terry McMillan for some late heroics. Place-kicker Henry Brown, however, appeared a most unlikely candidate.

Brown, a junior college transfer, shot down visiting Air Force with four field goals, including the game-winner with only 11 seconds remaining. His 30-yard boot passed through the uprights just 21 seconds after Air Force grabbed a 17-16 lead.

Coach Dan Devine's troops benefited from Devine and divine inspiration.

"I was a little down when we got the ball again with so little time left," Mizzou offensive tackle Mike Carroll told the *Columbia Missourian*. "Then I remembered a verse from Matthew: 'Oh men of little faith . . .'"

The Tigers also had hope anytime quarterback Terry McMillan stepped on the field.

McMillan put Brown in position for the clincher with a perfect 56-yard strike to John Henley. Everyone, including the Falcons, figured McMillan would look for the Missouri jet, Mel Gray. With Gray double-covered, McMillan launched the bomb to Henley, moving the Tigers from their own 24-yard line to the Air Force 20 with 24 seconds left.

After two running plays, Brown stepped on the field with 15 seconds to go. Eleven ticks remained when Brown's kick passed over the crossbar. The Tigers smothered their new kicking star before he could reach the sideline.

Brown's toe had been an Achilles heel the previous season when he missed 6 of 9 field goal attempts. He was even 0-for-3 in the Tigers' scrimmage one week before the 1969 opener.

Against Air Force, Brown missed his first attempt but then matched his 1968 total by halftime. His field goals from 42, 29, and 37 yards in the second quarter helped Mizzou forge a 16-7 lead at the half.

Statistically, the Tigers dominated the first half – 289 total yards to 84. But Ron McBride's 3-yard scoring run in the second quarter was Missouri's only touchdown of the day.

Air Force briefly held the lead at 7-0 after linebacker Phil Bauman scored on a 14-yard interception early in the second period.

Brown's game winner – his fourth 3-pointer of the game – shattered the school record. In fact, former coach and athletic director Don Faurot couldn't remember when a Tiger had kicked more than two field goals in a game. Brown's quartet of treys tied the Big Eight Conference record.

Tiger fans momentarily gulped on Brown's final try when Bob Wilson's snap from center sailed slightly high – ever so slightly. But McMillan fielded the ball and placed it perfectly for Brown.

"When the play started, I can't remember what I was thinking," Brown said.

Brown didn't want to know what the Falcons thought after he erased their miracle comeback.

Trailing 16-10 with 1:27 left in the game, Air Force faced fourth-and-21 at its own 20. Falcon quarterback Gary Baxter evaded a strong Tiger pass rush and hit end Mike Bolen for a 57-yard gain.

After a Tiger sack – Mizzou's eighth of the game – Baxter passed to end Charley Longnecker around the 2-yard line. Longnecker made the catch and pulled Missouri defensive back Butch Davis into the end zone with him.

Dennis Luethauser, who kicked four field goals in Air Force's upset of SMU a week earlier, nailed the tie-breaking extra point. That lead vanished a half minute later.

The *Missourian's* Doug Grow wrote this appraisal of the fourth quarter:

"More amazing than the Mets, more discouraging than a flunked final, more beautiful than Purple Mountain's Majesty and Raquel Welch in one stacked scene."

Missouri's ground attack, led by Joe Moore's 130 yards, quadrupled the Air Force rushing game (361-

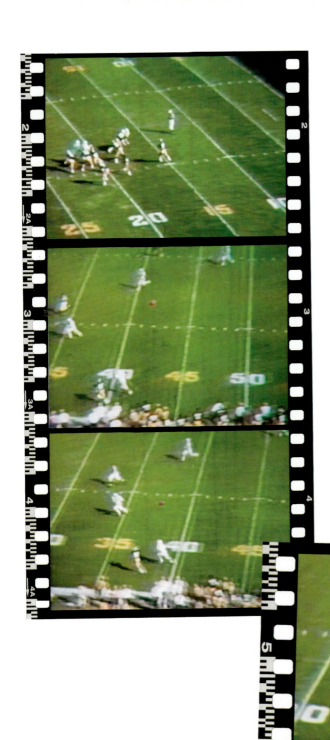

to-90). The Falcons, appropriately, had more air support (221-to-102).

Mistakes proved costly to both schools. Baxter's 67-yard touchdown pass was nullified by an illegal procedure penalty.

Missouri's Jon Staggers electrified the crowd with his 80-yard punt return but the officials pulled the plug – clipping. The Tigers fumbled away another scoring opportunity at the Air Force 5-yard line.

Seldom a walking quote machine, Missouri Coach Dan Devine may have issued one of the great understatements of his career:

"The best thing we did is that we didn't lose our poise."

And, one of the best things about the season opener – it set the stage for one of Missouri's finest seasons ever.

(Left, top to bottom) Terry McMillan's bomb to John Henley in the final half-minute set up the game-winning kick.

(Opposite) Henry Brown nailed four field goals, including the clincher with 11 seconds left.

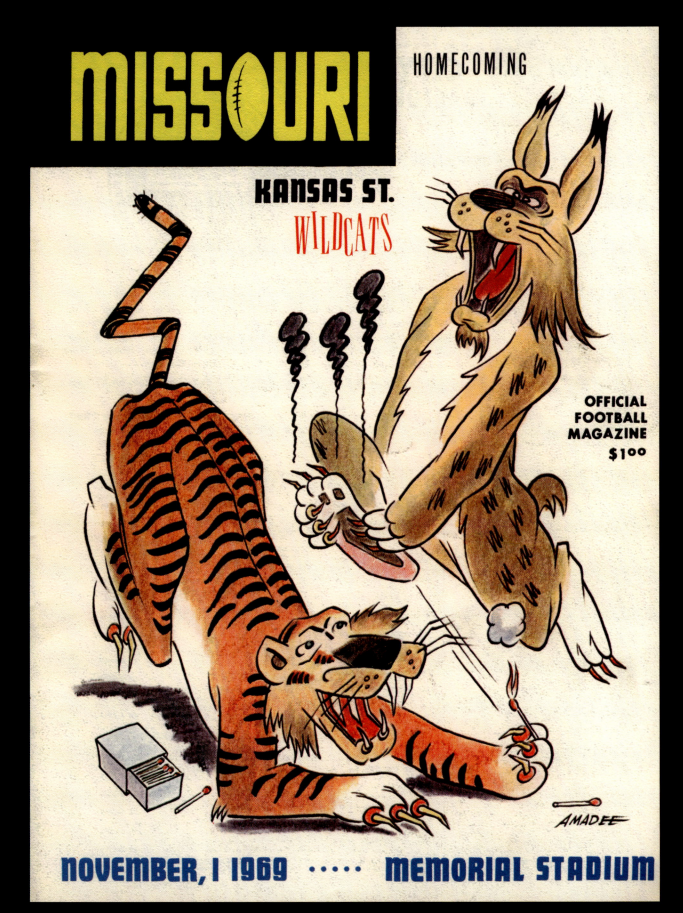

The 1969 Homecoming program cover

Missouri 41   Kansas State 38

Staggering!
NOVEMBER 1, 1969

Big Eight Conference Commissioner Wayne Duke called it "the greatest game I've ever seen."

Most of the 60,000 in attendance at Memorial Stadium in Columbia would agree with that assessment after watching Missouri and Kansas State slug it out in an offensive battle that showcased stars from both teams with record setting performances. The top performance was turned in by Missouri all-purpose back, receiver, return-man, and in this game, passer Jon Staggers.

Missouri dominated the first half. Quarterback Terry McMillan tossed two first quarter touchdown passes, a 19-yarder to Staggers, and a 5-yarder to tight end Tom Shryock to give Mizzou a 14-0 lead.

Kansas State made it a 14-6 game when Mack Herron scored on a 3-yard run early in the second quarter. It was Herron's first of four touchdowns on the day. The Tigers closed the first half scoring when Staggers threw a 4-yard halfback pass to Mel Gray for a touchdown. Mizzou led 21-6.

The Tigers benefited from a sub-par first half performance by Kansas State quarterback Lynn Dickey. Dickey completed just five of 18 passes for 52 yards in the first half. But, as fast as you could say "Holy Cow," (baseball play-by-play man Harry Caray was the special guest half time announcer) Dickey and the Wildcats turned the game around in the second half.

Midway in the third quarter, Dickey rallied the Wildcats with a 49-yard pass to John Duckers who took the ball to the 4-yard line. That set up a short touchdown run by Herron to cut the Tiger lead to 21-12.

No time for Kansas State to celebrate. On the ensuing kickoff, Staggers took the ball 99 yards for a touchdown to give Mizzou a 28-12 lead. Normally one would say that gave Missouri some breathing room, but there was no breathing room in this game. The pace of the game would only get faster. In fact, late in the third quarter, Kansas State scored the next two touchdowns in just seven seconds.

The first touchdown came on Herron's third short run of the day, climaxing an 80-yard

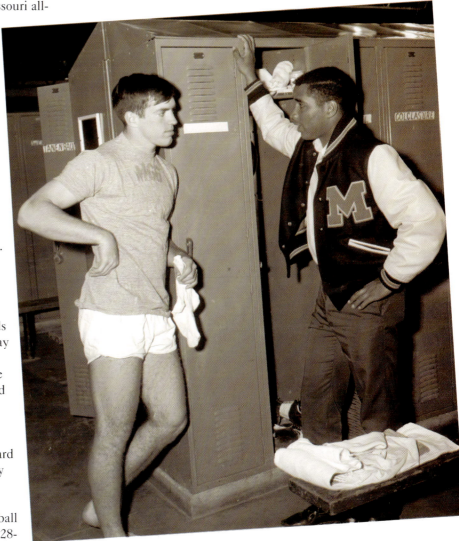

Roger Wehrli (left) and Jon Staggers were kick-returning threats as well as stellar performers on defense and offense.

Memorable Moments • 59

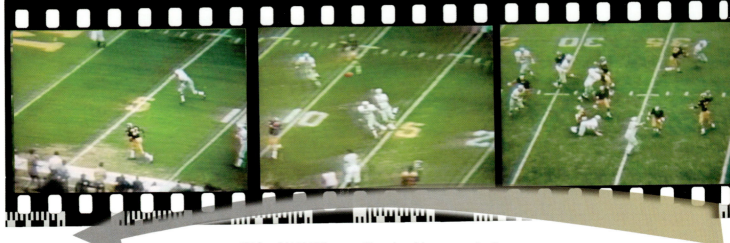

(Right to left) McMillan tosses 19-yard touchdown pass to Jon Staggers.

drive. K-State kicker Max Arreguin then lined up for the kickoff. As he approached the ball he bent over to tie his shoes. Missouri's receiving team relaxed, and Arreguin surprised everyone with an on-side kick. K-State recovered the kick at the Missouri 37-yard line. On the very next play, Dickey threw deep to receiver Charles Collins in the end zone for a touchdown. Two touchdowns in seven seconds and Kansas State closed the gap to 28-24.

As the fourth quarter began, momentum was definitely on Kansas State's side. The Wildcats moved through the Tiger defense with ease. They roared 80 yards in four plays, their touchdown drive capped by a 39-yard pass from Dickey to Collins. Kansas State led 31-28. Dickey and the Wildcats staggered Missouri. How appropriate that a player named Staggers would revive the staggering Tigers.

With 12:34 remaining in the game, the Tigers drove down the field. McMillan completed a 40-yard pass to John Henley at the Wildcat 16-yard line. Then Staggers took a pass to the 1-yard line. Ron McBride scored from there on a short run to put the Tigers back on top at 34-31.

The Tiger defense held the Wildcats on their next offensive possession, forcing a punt, and again the light shined on Jon Staggers. Staggers returned the punt up the middle for 40 yards to put the Tigers at the Wildcat 5-yard line. Four plays later, McMillan scored from the one and Mizzou led 41-31.

But in this game, no lead was safe with Lynn Dickey on the field. Dickey quickly passed the Wildcats down the field and cut into the Missouri lead with a 26-yard touchdown pass to Herron with 7:33 left in the game. For Herron it was his fourth touchdown in the game. For the Wildcats, they now trailed by just a field goal at 41-38.

In an offensive battle where the prevailing thought was whoever had the ball last would win, the defenses finally tightened up. The Tigers stopped Dickey and the Wildcats on their next drive, but Kansas State would have one last chance.

However, on a day when Dickey would set Big

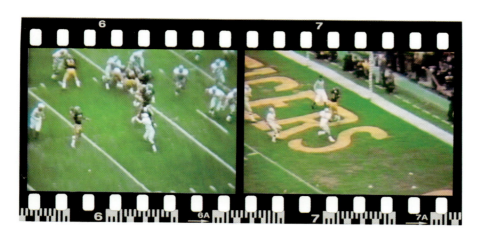

(Left to right) Staggers, on the halfback option, throws a 4-yard touchdown pass to Mel Gray.

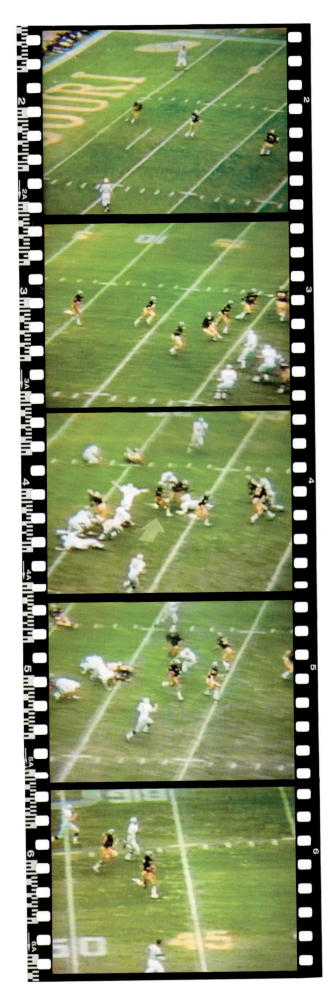

(Top to bottom) Staggers touched the ball 19 times for 295 yards against the Wildcats, including this 99-yard kickoff return.

Eight records for most total yards (394) and most passes thrown (49), his final pass was intercepted by Jerry Boyd with 1:29 left.

Missouri ran out the clock and held on for a heart-stopping 41-38 win.

The offensive numbers were impressive to say the least. Missouri's McMillan completed 12 of 22 passes for 223 yards. Joe Moore carried the ball 35 times for 144 yards.

But, the all-around play of Jon Staggers stood above the rest. He was named Big Eight Conference Back of the Week. He scored two touchdowns on a pass reception and a kickoff return, passed for another touchdown, and set up the eventual winning touchdown with a punt return. In all, Staggers handled the football 19 times for 295 yards. He modestly described his play as "fairly decent."

Missouri Coach Dan Devine was more emphatic: "Jon was the difference in the game."

Kansas State Coach Vince Gibson added, "Gee whiz, what a day he had!"

And Staggers himself summed it up by telling reporters after the game, "I just had a beautiful feeling about the game. We had to win it or we were through for the year."

The victory gave the Tigers a 6-and-1 record and put them in a three-way tie for first place in the conference with Kansas State and Nebraska. The win also moved Mizzou to ninth in the *Associated Press* Poll and set the stage for a 44-10 victory the next week against 20th ranked Oklahoma.

In that game, Staggers starred in front of his cousin who came to Columbia to watch the game. Staggers' cousin was tennis great Arthur Ashe.

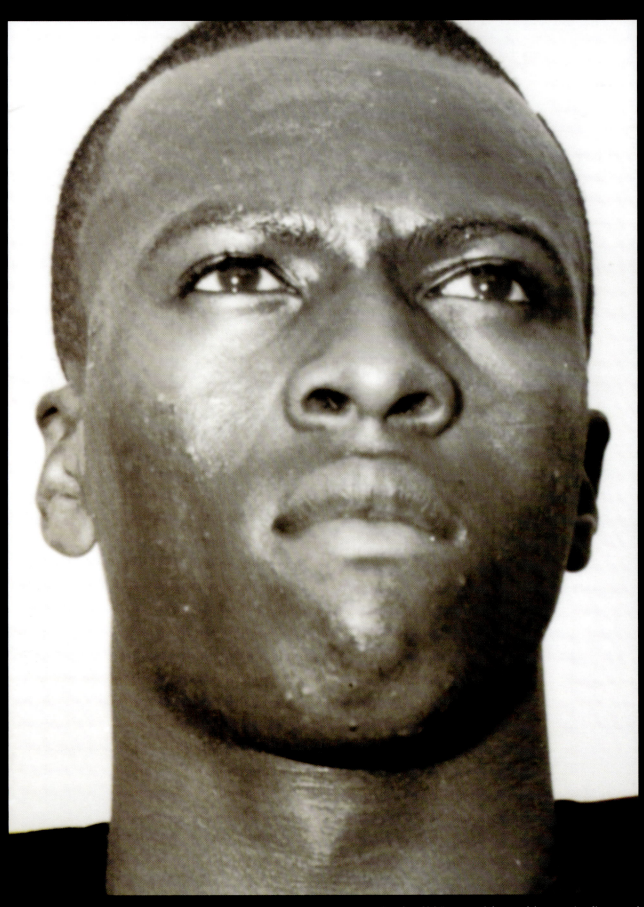

Speedster Mel Gray scored three touchdowns against Kansas and averaged 27 yards per reception during the 1969 season.

Missouri 69   Kansas 21

Tigers KO KU
NOVEMBER 22, 1969

The 1969 Missouri football team was arguably the greatest offensive team in Tiger history. As the season progressed, Mizzou's offense was like a runaway locomotive – it picked up steam.

In the final four games of the regular season, the Tigers scored 41 points against Kansas State, 44 points against Oklahoma, 40 points against Iowa State, and topped it off with an amazing 69-point effort against Kansas.

The only time a Mizzou football team scored more than 69 points in a game was back in 1907 when the Tigers beat Tarkio College, 70-6. But that was Tarkio and this was Kansas. Yes Kansas, the team that spoiled Missouri's national title hopes in 1960 with an upset victory in the final game of the season. Yes Kansas, the team that one year earlier beat Mizzou, 21-19.

Yes Kansas – enough said.

In 1969, the only thing that stood between Missouri and a share of the Big Eight Conference title and a trip to the Orange Bowl was Kansas. But, there would be no upset this season, only talk of Missouri running up the score against its dreaded rival.

The game was no contest. Before you could say Mel Gray, he scored on a 19-yard end around scamper. Just as quickly, Gray then hauled in a 63-yard touchdown pass from Terry McMillan. Follow that up with another McMillan touchdown pass to Jon Staggers, and the Tigers raced in front 21-0 at the end of the first quarter. Mizzou added one touchdown in the second quarter, a 26-yard touchdown pass from McMillan to Gray as the Tigers built a 28-7 halftime lead.

Any thoughts of a letdown for Missouri in the second half were quickly erased. The Tigers erupted for 28 points in the third quarter. Staggers caught a 6-yard touchdown pass from McMillan. Joe Moore followed with a 53-yard touchdown run. McMillan followed with two touchdown runs of his own – a 16-yarder and a 1-yarder.

The Tigers scored two more touchdowns in the fourth quarter including Staggers third score in the game. In all, 10 touchdowns for Missouri!

Mizzou converted on its first nine extra-point kicks before missing on the tenth, perhaps out of exhaustion. Final score: Missouri 69, Kansas 21.

The offensive numbers for Missouri were mind-boggling. The Tigers accounted for 30 first downs, 344 yards rushing, 307 yards passing. Gray scored three touchdowns; Staggers scored three touchdowns; McMillan tossed four touchdown passes and scored

(Right to left) Joe Moore (45) ran for 167 yards, including a 53-yard touchdown against the Jayhawks.

twice on the ground; and Moore added 167 yards rushing and a touchdown. With a performance like this, talk of Missouri running up the score was inevitable.

"I resent the insinuation that we were trying to run up the score," Missouri Coach Dan Devine told reporters after the game. "When I first came to Missouri we were getting beat 35-0, 45-0, and I never heard any talk about running up the score."

Kansas Coach Pepper Rodgers saw it differently: "I'm surprised they didn't throw it on the last play (of the game). I would have."

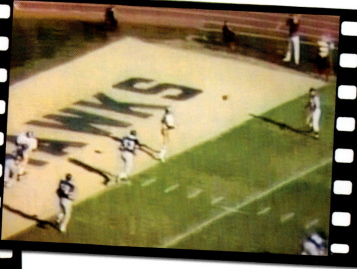

The game was actually more competitive in the stands than on the field. Late in the game, with Kansas hopelessly behind, a group of Jayhawk fans held up a sign that read:

"Kansas will be back."

Two Missouri students responded with a sign of their own:

"M.U. Orange Bowl. K.U. Toilet Bowl."

Jayhawk fans took exception with the Mizzou fans as both sides clashed in the seats behind the end zone. Police took the sign and escorted the Mizzou fans to safety.

(Top to bottom) Terry McMillan passes to Jon Staggers, who scored three touchdowns.

The Tiger fans were only repeating what the Kansas coach had already said. Prior to the game, Rodgers declared his team wasn't worthy for the "Toilet Bowl." In fact, some good-humored and perhaps disgusted Kansas fans threw toilet paper on the field.

In the end, one account had Rodgers acknowledging his total defeat to Devine saying, "I gave Dan the peace sign, and he gave half of it back to me."

The Tigers finished the regular season at 9-and-1, tied for the Big Eight Conference title with Nebraska. The only thing that could cool off the Tiger offense was time.

The Tigers had almost six weeks off before their next game, the Orange Bowl in Miami on January 1st. In that game the potent Mizzou offense could only score a field goal in a 10-3 loss to second-ranked Penn State. It was a disappointing finish to an otherwise spectacular Missouri football season – a season, which saw the Tigers finish with a 9-and-2 record and ranked sixth in the *Associated Press* poll.

(Top to bottom)McMillan tosses to Mel Gray, one of four TD passes on the day for McMillan.

Memorable Moments · 65

The front page of the South Bend Tribune *said it all.*

Missouri 30  Notre Dame 26

Al's Well That Ends Well
OCTOBER 21, 1972

Notre Dame had been such a prohibitive favorite against visiting Missouri the game was pulled from several football betting cards. The Tigers still gambled and won.

Six times they converted on fourth down – three for touchdowns – to present second-year Head Coach Al Onofrio with his first major victory.

"Even the heavens wept as Missouri pulled off the biggest upset of the 1972 college football season with a 30-26 triumph over the heavily favored Irish," wrote the *Indianapolis Star's* Ray Marquette.

The Irish, ranked seventh by *UPI*, also rated among the nation's best offensive and defensive teams. They drilled their first four opponents by a combined score of 130-30.

The Tigers, on the other hand, were licking their wounds after a 62-0 pasting by Nebraska the previous Saturday. The Cornhuskers inflicted both an emotional and physical beating at Lincoln. Several banged up Tigers were unable to suit up at Notre Dame.

But, with all odds against them, including a steady downpour under the Golden Dome, Missouri played nearly flawless football. The Tigers were turnover-free all afternoon while forcing four Irish miscues – two fumbles and two interceptions.

Before the Missouri visit, Notre Dame hadn't allowed a point in the first half – not a single point – in any game that season. Mizzou struck for 21 first-half points and, by the time it was over, had equaled the point production of Notre Dame's first four opponents.

"This is the biggest victory since I've been a coach at Missouri," Onofrio said.

Onofrio, who joined the Mizzou staff in 1958, assumed head coaching duties when Dan Devine fled for the Green Bay Packers after the 1970 season.

The transition, in terms of wins and losses, wasn't smooth. Missouri struggled to a 1-10 record in Onofrio's first season, the first 10-loss season in Mizzou history.

The 1972 season began on a brighter note as the Tigers split their first four games. Then came the annihilation at Nebraska. The oddsmakers rated Notre Dame as a four-to-five touchdown favorite.

In a classic case of role reversals, the Tigers

(Left to right) Bob Pankey (16) intercepts Irish quarterback Tom Clements (2) to set up Missouri's first touchdown.

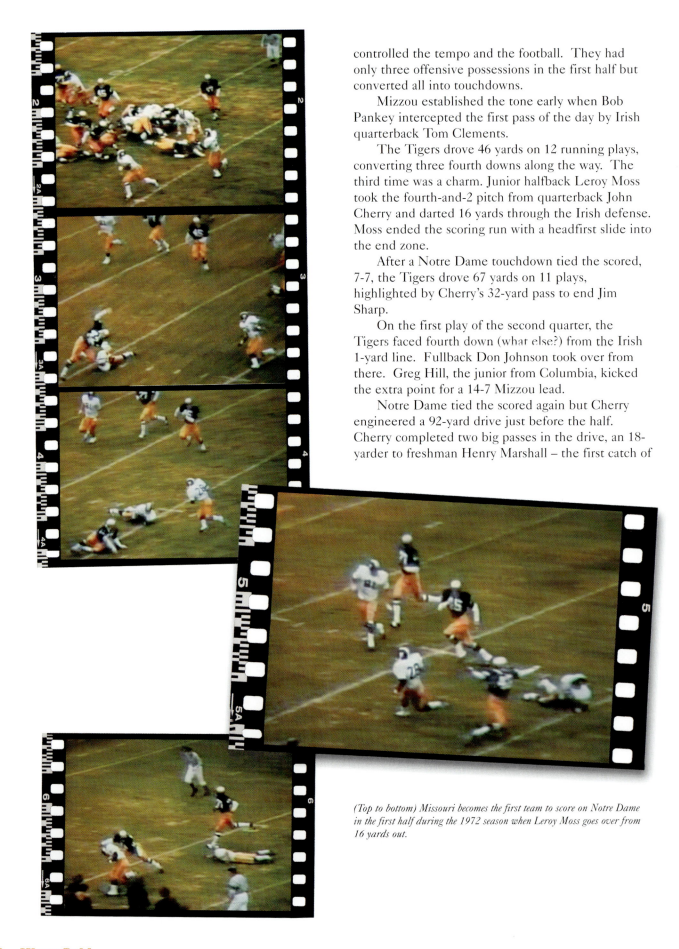

controlled the tempo and the football. They had only three offensive possessions in the first half but converted all into touchdowns.

Mizzou established the tone early when Bob Pankey intercepted the first pass of the day by Irish quarterback Tom Clements.

The Tigers drove 46 yards on 12 running plays, converting three fourth downs along the way. The third time was a charm. Junior halfback Leroy Moss took the fourth-and-2 pitch from quarterback John Cherry and darted 16 yards through the Irish defense. Moss ended the scoring run with a headfirst slide into the end zone.

After a Notre Dame touchdown tied the scored, 7-7, the Tigers drove 67 yards on 11 plays, highlighted by Cherry's 32-yard pass to end Jim Sharp.

On the first play of the second quarter, the Tigers faced fourth down (what else?) from the Irish 1-yard line. Fullback Don Johnson took over from there. Greg Hill, the junior from Columbia, kicked the extra point for a 14-7 Mizzou lead.

Notre Dame tied the scored again but Cherry engineered a 92-yard drive just before the half. Cherry completed two big passes in the drive, an 18-yarder to freshman Henry Marshall – the first catch of

(Top to bottom) Missouri becomes the first team to score on Notre Dame in the first half during the 1972 season when Leroy Moss goes over from 16 yards out.

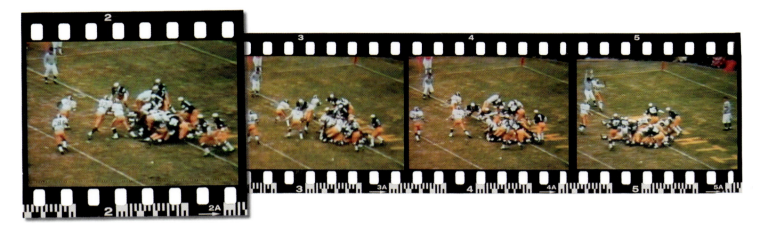

(Left to right) Don Johnson added two one-yard touchdown runs. Tommy Reamon makes his high-five "official."

his stellar career at Missouri – and a 31-yarder to fullback Bill Ziegler. The Tigers didn't always wait until fourth down. They successfully converted on three third-down plays.

Ziegler's reception moved Mizzou to the Notre Dame 7-yard line.

Four plays later – yes, fourth down – Johnson edged over again for a 1-yard TD.

Even the Irish joined in on the Tigers' fourth down conversion spree. During the 92-yard drive Notre Dame tackle Greg Marx jumped offside on Jack Bastable's punt. The first half's only penalty was enough for a drive-sustaining first down.

Missouri controlled the ball for nearly 20 minutes of the opening half en route to a 21-14 lead.

In the third quarter Notre Dame fumbled a punt and a kickoff, leading to a pair of Greg Hill field goals.

"I don't know why we fumbled so much," Irish coach Ara Parseghian said. "The ball was just as wet for both sides."

Missouri carried a 27-14 lead into the fourth quarter and tacked on three more points.

Hill capped a 73-yard drive with his third field goal of the game. Tommy Reamon's 29-yard run and a Notre Dame pass interference penalty were key plays in the Tigers' final scoring march. Missouri led, 30-14, with 10:13 left in the game.

The Irish finally woke up. Clements scored on a 13-yard keeper with 7:37 remaining but John Moseley broke up Clements' 2-point pass attempt. Missouri 30, Notre Dame 20.

With 4:10 to go, Irish fullback Andy Huff scored on a 12-yard run but the Tigers stuffed Huff on a 2-point running attempt. Missouri 30, Notre Dame 26.

With 2:37 to play, Notre Dame took possession on its own 13. Missouri's Mike Fink stepped in front of a Clements pass and returned the interception to the Irish 15.

Cherry tried to run out the clock but Notre Dame got the ball back once more, this time with only two seconds remaining. Clements fumbled the ball during a frantic scramble as time expired.

"It feels like we just won a bowl game," Johnson said.

A bowl wasn't far off. Missouri surprised Colorado one week after Notre Dame. The Tigers finished the regular season with a 6-5 record and received an invitation to the Fiesta.

The miracle at Notre Dame undoubtedly influenced the bowl selection committee but Mizzou fans probably remember that game more prominently as the first of the incredible upsets from the Onofrio era.

Noseguard Herris Butler smothers a Nebraska field goal attempt in the third quarter to keep the score tied, 6-6.

Missouri 13   Nebraska 12

The Butler Did It
OCTOBER 13, 1973

The only stat that counts is the final score. Truer words were never spoken when considering Mizzou's 13-12 upset of Nebraska in 1973. The Huskers dominated the game in first downs and total yards. But, when it came to the kicking game and making big plays at crucial moments, the Tigers won that battle as well as the game.

Missouri and Nebraska entered the 1973 game with identical 4-0 records. Nebraska was ranked second, Missouri 12th. There was one other pre-game factor. Missouri had a score to settle – literally.

The season before, Nebraska beat the Tigers in Lincoln 62-0! So, revenge and payback were factors for Missouri in this game. And, this game was not in Lincoln. This game was played before a record crowd of 68,170 on a beautiful fall afternoon at Faurot Field.

This much anticipated conference opener for both teams was actually a yawner for the first half. The Tigers and the Huskers traded field goals – two by Nebraska's Rich Sanger, and two by Mizzou's Greg Hill – that made the score 6-6 at halftime. But, a pattern had developed in this game – a pattern that would hold true for the second half.

Missouri won the battle of field position. Throughout the game, Mizzou punter Jim Goble pinned Nebraska deep in its own territory. The Huskers tried to battle their way out from near their own goal line, but Mizzou's defense eventually stopped them and forced Nebraska to punt. This pattern, this strategy worked so well that the Tigers – outgained in total yards (444-170) and in first downs (21-7) – remained in the game.

Now enter the heroics of Missouri noseguard Herris Butler. Butler was an undersized defensive lineman at 5-11 and 218 pounds, but was cat quick and spent a good portion of his day busting through the Nebraska offensive line.

Late in the third quarter, Nebraska drove to the Missouri 4-yard line. Faced with fourth and goal, Nebraska Coach Tom Osborne elected to go for the field goal. Prior to the snap, Butler jumped offside. The penalty moved the ball to the 2-yard line. With the scored tied 6-6 and locked in a defensive struggle, Osborne and the Huskers still elected to go for the field goal. That's when Butler atoned for his offside penalty in a big way.

"I really got mad and I told myself I'm going to block that ball," Butler said after the game.

Butler made good on his promise. He surged right through the middle of the Nebraska line and smothered Sanger's chip shot field goal to keep the game at a 6-6 tie.

"I just twisted my body a little bit and got through the seam somehow. I'll probably never do it again in a million years," Butler added.

Once again, even though Nebraska was able to move the ball on

Center Scott Anderson snapped the ball and recovered the crucial fumbled punt.

Memorable Moments • 71

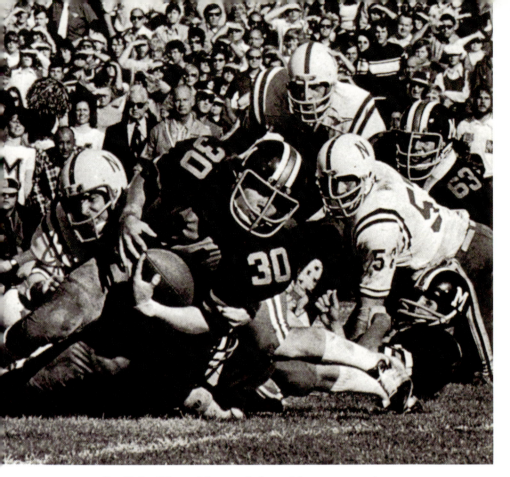

Tom Mulkey (30) scored the game-winning touchdown on a one-yard run.

offense, Missouri turned the Huskers away with no points to show for their efforts. Butler's blocked field goal set the stage for a fourth quarter that featured more big plays at crucial moments for the Tigers.

With two-and-a-half minutes left in the game and the scored still tied 6-6, Missouri was forced to punt from its 46-yard line. Once again, Jim Goble delivered a punt deep into Nebraska territory. Husker return man Randy Borg retreated inside his 10-yard line.

He could have called for a fair catch.

He could have let the ball roll into the end zone for a touchback.

Instead, Borg went for the return.

"This one was right in the pocket. I just tried to run too soon. I debated for a moment whether to call for a fair catch and decided not to," Borg said.

His decision proved costly for Nebraska. Missouri All-American center Scott Anderson, who snapped the ball on the play, was the first player down the field for Mizzou to cover the punt.

"I snapped the ball and nobody held me up," Anderson told reporters after the game. "I went down the field and nobody touched me. The guy caught the ball, and then he juggled it and went to his knees. The ball was just there. I went for it and was fortunate enough to get it. It's a great thrill for a lineman."

Missouri now had the ball at the Nebraska 4-yard line. Junior fullback Tom Mulkey took a handoff and went over the right side for three yards to the 1-yard line. On the next play he crashed over the goal line for a touchdown with 2:03 to play. Hill added the extra point and Missouri had its first lead of the day at 13-6.

But, two minutes to play was plenty of time for Nebraska to tie or win the game. Husker quarterback David Humm quickly passed Nebraska down the field. He completed a 31-yard pass to Rich Bahe and a 20-yarder to Larry Mushinskie. After a handoff to running back Tony Davis that lost a yard, Humm hit Bahe on a pattern across the middle for a 22-yard touchdown. Seventy-two yards in just four plays. Nebraska trailed 13-12 with one minute to play.

Osborne and Nebraska didn't hesitate. They refused to settle for the tie, opting instead for the two-point conversion and the win. Humm, a left-handed quarterback, rolled to his left and fired the ball toward Davis who was at the goal line. Mizzou

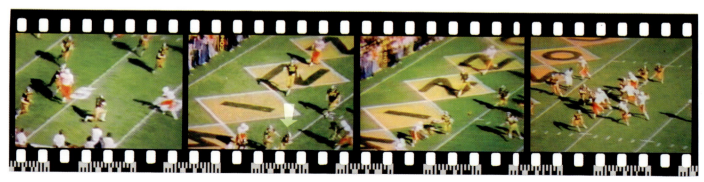

(Right to left) Nebraska's 2-point conversion attempt: Tiger defensive end Bob McRoberts tips David Humm's pass. Tony Gillick intercepts to preserve Mizzou's upset.

Head Coach Al Onofrio gets a ride off the field.

defender Bob McRoberts tipped the ball just enough for Tony Gillick to step in front of Davis for the interception and preserve the 13-12 lead.

"I was looking for that exact play," Gillick said. "I knew they'd throw, but I didn't know which way. Humm throws better going to his left, so I just cheated over that way a little."

Osborne defended his play selection: "It was probably as good a percentage play as we had. If I had it to do over though, I would have called time out and thought about two or three other possible plays."

Missouri ran out the clock and held on for a 13-12 upset over the second-ranked Cornhuskers. Fans stormed the field. The north goalpost came down.

Missouri Coach Al Onofrio: "What a day! It's just a great day! I've had a lot of teams in the past play hard as they knew how, but this team played harder than it knew it could."

Nebraska Coach Tom Osborne: "Missouri had lots going psychologically, and they played a very emotional game. We just couldn't overcome the mistakes we made."

Missouri noseguard Herris Butler: "It feels real good to win though, no matter what the score...this paid them back for the last three years."

Missouri center Scott Anderson: "It's the greatest thrill of my life. I said that after the Notre Dame game too, but this is it. Any more thrills like this and I'll have ulcers."

The victory moved the Tigers to seventh in the *Associated Press* poll. Unfortunately, Missouri lost four of its last five games during the 1973 season and finished with a 7-4 record. The Tigers capped the season with a 34-17 win over Auburn in the Sun Bowl.

Still, when Tiger fans think about the 1973 season, they remember that beautiful October day at Faurot Field and the heroics of Butler, McRoberts, Gillick, Anderson, Goble, Mulkey and the rest. Mizzou fans would have to savor the win, because it would be 30 years before the next victory over Nebraska at Faurot Field.

The Faurot Field scoreboard tells it all.

The sign at Faurot Field shows the Tigers' murderous 1975 schedule.

74 • MizzouRah!

Missouri 20   Alabama 7

Turning the Tide
SEPTEMBER 8, 1975

Paul "Bear" Bryant and Ara Parseghian must have had flashbacks. On this Monday night at Birmingham's Legion Field, Bryant – while walking the sidelines prior to the Missouri matchup – sensed his Alabama players weren't quite ready for the Tigers. The "Bear" might have hearkened back to that late December evening in 1968 when Mizzou "horsewhipped" his Crimson Tide.

Parseghian – the former Notre Dame coach in the broadcast booth for his first game as an ABC-TV color commentator – certainly remembered the last time he personally viewed Missouri as a huge underdog. The Tigers clawed Parseghian's Irish on a rainy afternoon in South Bend during the 1972 season.

History aside, this figured to be Alabama's showcase. The Crimson Tide, ranked second to Oklahoma in the pre-season polls, had won 43 of its last 44 regular season games.

"Bear Bryant thinks he may have the best team of his already illustrious career," wrote the *Washington Post's* Paul Attner. "The only team on Alabama's schedule that appears strong enough to handle Bryant's men is Auburn."

ABC didn't give Al Onofrio's Tigers much of a chance, either. But the network hoped to fill the gap between pro football's exhibition and regular season with this prime time college contest. Even if the Tigers couldn't compete with the Tide, the game telecast might cut into "All in the Family's" Monday night premiere on CBS.

Back in Columbia, a number of classes let out early in attempts to give the university students and faculty ample time to prepare.

Even the most ardent Tiger fans weren't fully prepared for the incredible performance they were about to watch.

Mizzou, a three-touchdown underdog, tamed the Tide. The Tiger defense, led by tackles Keith Morrissey and Randy Frisch, held the usually potent Alabama offense to 3 yards on its first nine plays. Missouri limited the Crimson Tide to only 56 yards in the first two quarters.

"A lot of that credit goes to Al Onofrio," Morrissey said. "We were preparing for that game way back in the spring. They were traditionally a wishbone running team that just pounded it out with big lineman and talented running backs. Coach Onofrio developed a defense to take that away from them."

The offense did its job, too, scoring on four of its first five possessions for a 20-0 halftime lead.

After stopping Alabama's first offensive series, the Tigers marched 58 yards on 12 plays. Tailback

Tony Galbreath, alternating power with agility, rushed for 48 yards on nine carries during the drive. Galbreath's 3-yard touchdown burst through a huge hole put Missouri on top, 7-0, midway through the first quarter.

On their next possession, the Tigers "settled" for Tim Gibbons' 44-yard field goal and a 10-0 first quarter lead. Mizzou matched that scoring output in the second quarter.

After Mizzou safety Jim Leavitt recovered a Tide fumble at the Alabama 32, Missouri cashed in on a 9-yard touchdown run by fullback John Blakeman. Mizzou led, 17-0.

After Tiger safety Ken Downing intercepted a Richard Todd pass, Missouri's offense went to work again. Galbreath, who rushed for 89 yards in the first half, proved he could throw, too. Galbreath connected with Joe Stewart for 11 yards and a first down.

Gibbons, whose longest career field goal was the 44-yarder he nailed in the first quarter, added two more yards to his personal best. His 46-yarder deflected off the left upright and bounced over the crossbar. Missouri 20, Alabama ZERO.

Missouri's offensive domination in the first half included a 20-0 scoreboard advantage, 8-of-11 third down conversions (Bama was 0-for-5 on third downs), and 179 yards of total offense to a meager 56 yards for

(Top to bottom) Tiger defensive back Bruce Carter (2) forces an Alabama fumble.

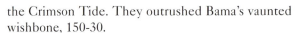

the Crimson Tide. They outrushed Bama's vaunted wishbone, 150-30.

Fans back in Missouri screamed their approval to TV sets. In Missouri's Legion Field locker room Onofrio was speechless.

"I just sat there and thought, 'That's about the best half of football I've ever seen a Missouri team play,'" Onofrio recounted. "The team was still so

(Right to left) Tony Galbreath climbs over the Alabama front line on this 3-yard touchdown. Galbreath rushed for 89 yards in the first half.

high in the dressing room that it was difficult to talk to them. So I didn't say a word. I just let 'em holler and keep their emotion."

ABC eventually got the message: Missouri was in command.

"I remember (sideline reporter) Jim Lampley on the sideline with a little utility truck and crane," Morrissey said. "They kept it behind the Alabama bench for the first half. Then they realized they needed to swing that truck over behind our bench."

The Tigers couldn't continue to roll the Tide, at least not so convincingly. Alabama ended its scoring drought in the fourth quarter. After a Missouri fumble, Todd completed three straight passes, ending with a 14-yard TD toss to All-American end Ozzie Newsome. The Tigers even had a hand on that one. Safety Bruce Carter partially tipped Todd's pass before Newsome pulled it in.

Trailing 20-7 with 10:24 left in the game, Alabama had a flicker of hope. Missouri quickly snuffed out the Tide's prospects. Morrissey, an undersized lineman at 218 pounds, emerged as the game's defensive star with three second-half sacks.

"They had those big lineman who used to get into a four-point stance and bulldoze forward," said Morrissey, a former high school quarterback. "In the second half, they realized they couldn't break our defense and had to go into a passing mode. Those big ol' boys had to get into a three-point stance and they weren't that agile. That suited my style. I just gave them a fake and they couldn't move their feet."

Alabama's offense was only slightly more productive in the second half. The Tide managed only 118 yards of total offense for the game. Alabama's running game, traditionally one of the country's best, was virtually nonexistent – 31 yards on 34 carries.

"All in all, it was a good 'ol country beating," Bryant said. "I think we were fortunate not to be beaten worse."

Morrissey was the Chevrolet Defensive Player of the Game. Galbreath, who finished with 120 yards on 32 rushing attempts, was the offensive MVP.

After the game the Missouri campus was flooded with hundreds of students who joined in an impromptu celebration and victory parade. They jammed Columbia streets and choked roads leading to the airport.

"That airport was just engulfed with fans; it was crazy," Morrissey said. "But it was an enormous experience just to see the support and how much people really appreciate a victory like that."

Missouri fans would later prove how much they appreciate a maximum effort, win or lose.

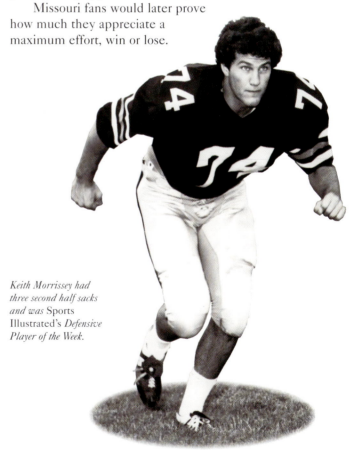

Keith Morrissey had three second half sacks and was Sports Illustrated's *Defensive Player of the Week.*

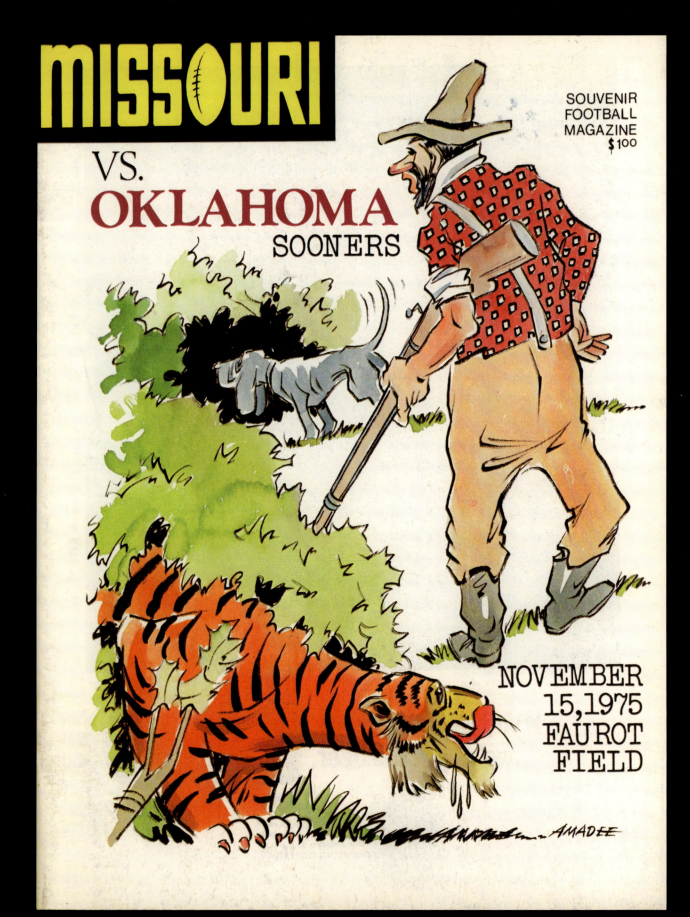

The 1975 Missouri vs. Oklahoma program cover

Missouri 27 — Oklahoma 28

Standing-O
NOVEMBER 15, 1975

Almost numb, they stood and applauded – a then-record crowd of 69,733 at Faurot Field.

The fans, prominently Mizzou Black and Gold with a sprinkling of Sooner red, were emotionally spent. The game was over, but they weren't quite ready to leave, not before one final tribute for a supreme effort in one of the most incredible college football games ever witnessed.

Missouri fans were in no mood for celebrations. Their Tigers had come up short – oh, so short – on the scoreboard. Oklahoma diehards, though, weren't ready to whoop it up. They knew they had survived, not conquered.

The Tigers had roared back after a 20-0 halftime deficit. The defending national champion Sooners, just a week earlier, had fumbled away their game to Kansas. That was the first loss for third-year Coach Barry Switzer and ended Oklahoma's 37-game unbeaten string.

Mizzou fans had grown accustomed to knocking off the big boys under Head Coach Al Onofrio. Notre Dame, Colorado, Nebraska, Arizona State and – in the 1975 season – Alabama all fell to Missouri.

Not Oklahoma, though. Not with an aggregation of talent which included Washington, Peacock, Davis, Owens, and Selmon – everywhere a Selmon.

Plus, you just don't go spotting 20 points to the Sooners.

But the Tigers did exactly that and still almost pulled it off – almost.

In the second half Missouri ran through and passed over Oklahoma like no team in recent history. The Tigers ripped the Sooners for 318 total yards and scored 27 straight points in the second half.

Missouri took a 21-20 lead with 8:33 left in the game and extended the Tiger advantage to 27-20 with 5:38 left to play.

You could never count out the Sooners, especially with one backfield position occupied by Joe Washington, who Switzer called his "greatest player ever."

With less than five minutes left in the game, Washington took a fourth-and-one handoff from the Sooners' 29 and raced 71 yards for a touchdown. Washington then eked into the end zone (officially, anyway) for the 2-point conversion and a 28-27 Oklahoma lead.

The Tigers still refused to go quietly. Mizzou quarterback Steve Pisarkiewicz flipped a screen pass to tailback Tony Galbreath, who rambled 45 yards to the Oklahoma 20.

Four plays later Tim Gibbons' 40-yard field goal try never had a chance.

"Someone smiled on us today," Switzer said, his voice cracking. "There were two great football teams out there."

Sooner quarterback Steve Davis, an ordained Baptist minister, could barely speak after the game but acknowledged, "I've never played in a greater game than this."

Tiger quarterback Steve Pisarkiewicz passed for 268 yards, most of them during Mizzou's second half comeback

Wide receiver Henry Marshall made six catches for 199 yards.

The game wasn't such a classic at the beginning, other than classic Sooner domination.

With Davis directing the Wishbone attack, Oklahoma scored on two first quarter touchdown runs – a 25-yarder by Elvis Peacock after a lateral from Davis and 3-yarder by Washington.

With 24 seconds left in the half, Davis squeezed into the end zone on a 1-yard keeper. Peacock's 2-point conversion run gave the Sooners a seemingly insurmountable 20-0 lead. The OU signal caller rushed for 107 yards on 11 first half carries.

The Sooner offense, which committed eight turnovers against Kansas and fumbled 13 turnovers the previous week against Iowa State, played error-free football against the Tigers all day.

Missouri's offense showed signs of life but misfired at inopportune moments. Tiger quarterback Steve Pisarkiewicz, admittedly a bit "hyper" in the early going, threw an interception on his first pass of the day.

Late in the second quarter, "Zark" hooked up with Henry Marshall, who made a brilliant 39-yard reception. A Pisarkiewicz fumble killed the scoring chance at the OU 30.

Missouri looked like a different team in the second half. On the Tigers' first possession Pisarkiewicz hit Marshall with a perfect strike, a 50-yard gain to the Oklahoma 3-yard line. Galbreath's 3-yard plunge and Gibbons' point-after trimmed the OU lead to 20-7 after three quarters.

The Tigers were unstoppable in the fourth quarter. It was Pisarkiewicz to Marshall again, this time 41 yards to the Sooner 33.

From there it was the Curtis Brown show. Brown needed only two carries to reach the end zone: a 10-yard cutback and a 23-yard sweep around left end. Another point-after by Gibbons trimmed the Sooner lead to six points at 20-14.

The overflow crowd went into full-time standing mode for the rest of the game.

Carrying Oklahoma defenders with him, Brown gained 8 and 19 yards on consecutive carries to spark the Tigers to a 46-yard touchdown drive. Brown, splitting time with an ailing Galbreath, would finish the afternoon with 153 yards on 20 carries.

Galbreath was well enough to score again from the 3. Gibbons' kick gave Mizzou its first lead, 21-20, with 8:33 left in the game.

After an Oklahoma punt Missouri took possession in Sooner territory. A holding penalty put the Tigers in a third-and-25 situation at the OU 40. Pisarkiewicz faked pass and then handed to Brown for a draw play up the middle. Brown found a big hole in the Sooner line and cut toward the left sideline. The Sooners finally caught Brown around the 2-yard line and forced the Tiger back to fumble.

The ball squirted into the end zone. Tiger end Randy Grossart pounced on it for the touchdown. Gibbons, who had hit on 29 straight extra points, missed this one. Missouri led, 27-20, with 5:38 left in the game.

Gibbons' kickoff sailed into the end zone for a touchback. From their own 20 the Sooners tried three running plays. Davis picked up 3 yards on first down. Mizzou held Washington to 2 yards on second down. On third down Peacock gained 4 yards but Mizzou cornerback Kenny Downing stopped him short of the first down marker.

On the Oklahoma sideline Switzer made the

A record crowd stood for the entire fourth quarter and well after the game.

decision to go for it, in all likelihood an all or nothing choice.

A presence on the Missouri sideline, though, may have been equally decisive.

Downing, Missouri's leading tackler – Missouri's SUREST tackler – had nursed a painful shoulder injury much of the season. Summoned to the sidelines after the Peacock stop, Downing was a spectator for the fourth-and-one try.

Even the most die-hard Tiger fans weren't expecting the near impossible. Stopping the Sooners short with only a yard to go? That was too much to ask.

Tiger fans may have been willing to concede one yard. That simply wasn't enough to satisfy Joe Washington.

With Downing watching, Washington took an option pitch from Davis, ran past Downing's replacement, turned on the jets and blasted 71 yards for the touchdown.

Whether Downing would have made the tackle is pure conjecture. Years later, Washington acknowledged the Sooners were aware of his absence and proceeded accordingly.

Downing was back on the field as Switzer gambled again. Rather than play it safe with a tying kick, the Sooners would go for two.

Again Washington got the call on a virtual replay of the touchdown. This time Downing was there to meet him. Downing forced Washington wide and brought down the shifty halfback near the goal line – over the line according to the official – short by Tiger reckoning.

"I don't think he made it," Downing said. "I know his hip hit the six-inch line and he bounced in."

Washington, whose talents as a football player might be exceeded by his class as a person, would not get dragged into a controversy.

"I thought I got into the end zone but it was close," Washington said. "I can understand Missouri being upset."

Now trailing, 28-27, the Tigers weren't prepared to pack it in. After the Oklahoma kickoff, Mizzou took possession at its own 16-yard line. Pisarkiewicz completed a pair of third down passes, the first to Marshall followed by Galbreath's 45-yard scoot off the screen pass.

With possession at the Oklahoma 20, Missouri lost yardage on three straight running plays, setting the stage for Gibbons' 40-yard attempt.

The wind was at his back but nothing short of a hurricane would have helped this one. The ball bounced to the turf well short of the goal posts.

Missouri got the ball back once more, with time enough for one play. A 54-yard field goal attempt by Gibbons also fell well short of its mark.

The crowd, still on its feet, did not hasten to the exits. Instead, they waited to pay a final tribute to two teams – especially their Tigers – who left it all on the field.

"That was the best game I've ever played in my life," Marshall said. "We made 'em earn it."

And how.

Missouri defensive back Kenny Downing wrapped up Joe Washington on this run, but was out for the game's pivotal play.

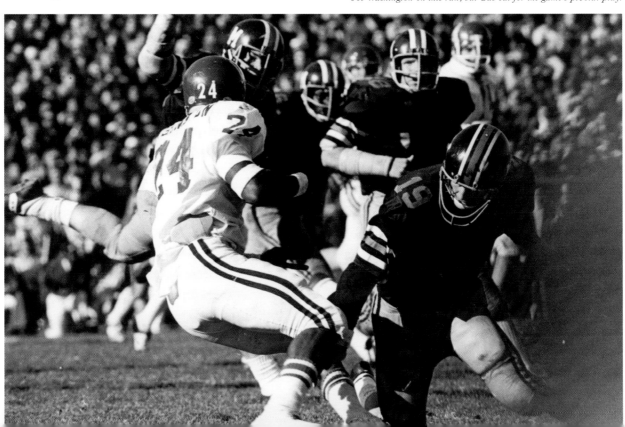

The Trojans featured Heisman candidate Ricky Bell on the program cover but...
(Courtesy USC)

Missouri 46   USC 25

Trojans Fed to Tigers at Coliseum
SEPTEMBER 11, 1976

For the second straight year, Missouri opened the season on the road against a top-10 ranked opponent. In 1975, the Tigers dismantled second-ranked Alabama. In 1976, Missouri traveled west to Southern California to take on the eighth-ranked Trojans at the Coliseum in Los Angeles.

Just like the year before, everything seemed to be stacked against the Tigers. But, just like the year before, Missouri came away with a shocking season-opening upset.

What exactly were the obstacles facing the Tigers for this road opener against USC? It was a night game, two time zones west of Columbia, against an opponent with one of the most storied programs in college football. The game was played in the Los Angeles Memorial Coliseum, where the Trojans enjoyed a tremendous home field advantage at one of the most historic of all sporting venues.

Missouri starting quarterback Steve Pisarkiewicz cut his finger earlier in the week and the Tiger coaching staff wasn't certain if "Zark" would play, or if backup quarterback Pete Woods would be the signal caller.

Now, add in the weather. On the day before and morning of the game, Los Angeles experienced a rare tropical storm, Kathleen. As the song goes: "It never rains in Southern California?" Well, it poured, leaving the Tigers without a chance to practice on Friday and a sloppy field for the game on Saturday night. The wet field was seen as an advantage for USC and its running game led by Heisman Trophy candidate Ricky Bell.

Now, add in a new coach. John Robinson was making his head coaching debut for USC after taking over for longtime Trojan legend, Coach John McKay.

So the eighth-ranked Trojans were loaded with talent, with a new coach, a wet field, and a vaunted running game against a questionable Tiger run defense.

However, Missouri controlled this game from the

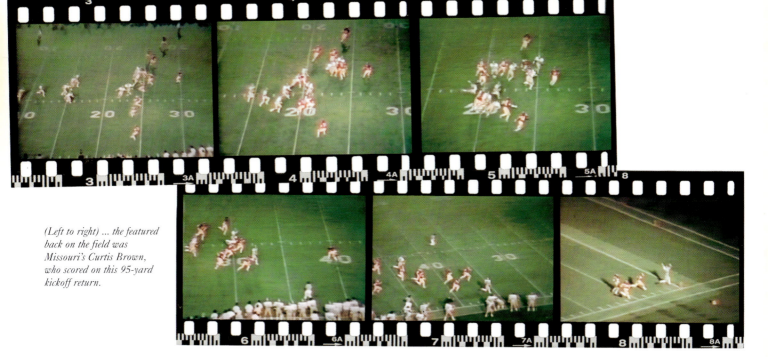

(Left to right) ... the featured back on the field was Missouri's Curtis Brown, who scored on this 95-yard kickoff return.

Memorable Moments • 83

start. After stopping USC on its first possession, the Trojans' long snapper hiked the ball over the punter's head and Missouri took over at the USC 21-yard line. Four plays later, Tiger running back Curtis Brown scored on a short run to give Mizzou a 7-0 lead.

USC responded with an 84-yard drive on 12 plays. Bell dominated – running for 49 yards on the drive including the last six yards for a touchdown to tie the game 7-7.

But the star running back in this game would not be Ricky Bell. The star running back in this game emerged during the next 11 seconds. Curtis Brown took the ensuing kickoff and returned it 95 yards for a touchdown to give Missouri a 13-7 lead. The play showed the Tigers' explosiveness. It also showed that Mizzou would not roll over against the favored Trojans.

The Tigers and Trojans traded a couple of field goals before Missouri flexed its offensive muscle late in the first half. Pisarkiewicz drove the Tigers 78 yards in nine plays, the final 25 yards on a touchdown pass to Leo Lewis. Tigers led, 23-10, with 2:15 to go in the first half.

USC couldn't move the ball and Missouri got it back for one last drive in the final minute. Brown took a short swing pass from Pisarkiewicz and turned it into a spectacular 49-yard touchdown. Brown broke several tackles as he zigzagged his way to the end zone for a 30-10 Missouri halftime lead.

The Tigers didn't sit on their lead. They expanded it, and impressively so. Midway in the third quarter, Mizzou marched 81 yards for another score on Leo Lewis' 24-yard reverse. The Tigers now led 39-10 and the game was over for the USC fans who headed for the exits. Those who stayed saw a glimpse of the future as freshman running back Charles White, an eventual Heisman Trophy winner, scored two consolation touchdowns. Final score: Missouri 46, USC 25.

It was the most one-sided loss in an opening game in USC football history.

Longtime *Los Angeles Times* writer Mal Florence called USC's defeat "one of the most stunning losses in Trojan football history – considering the size of the score and that USC was favored to win the Pacific Eight title."

For the second straight year, Missouri opened its season with an impressive road win against one of college football's most storied programs.

For Missouri Coach Al Onofrio, the victory at the Coliseum was extra sweet. As a high school football player in Los Angeles he played in an all-star game at the Coliseum, and was a hot dog vendor there during USC and UCLA games from 1936 to 1938.

Onofrio's teams were beginning to be recognized as the upset monsters of college football. USC's Bell rushed for 172 yards but was still upstaged by Brown, who ran for 101 yards and scored three touchdowns – one running, one receiving, and one on a kickoff return. He had a fourth touchdown called back because of a penalty.

"Bell is a great back," Onofrio told reporters after the game, "but there is no better running back in the country than Brown, and best thing about Brown is, he's mine."

With Brown leading the way, Mizzou outgained the Trojans 315-298 on the ground.

Most Tiger fans back in Columbia remember watching the game on a one-hour tape delayed telecast. However, a special closed circuit live showing of the game took place at the Hearnes Center, where about 300 fans showed up to watch the game on a giant TV screen.

The victory sparked a celebration as the streets in Columbia around the campus filled with students and fans. A large group of several hundred fans gathered at Faurot Field to tear down the goalposts, but University police were successful in turning the crowd away with the goalposts intact. The students moved from there to the airport, where they, and members of Marching Mizzou, greeted the team at six o'clock Sunday morning.

Years later, Robinson recalled his first game as Trojan head coach by saying the Missouri squad was one of the finest offensive teams he ever faced during his long and illustrious coaching career. In fact, the only loss Robinson suffered during his first season as head coach at USC was to Mizzou. The Trojans won their next 11 games, including the Rose Bowl, and finished ranked second in the nation.

After such an impressive start, the Tigers finished the season with a lackluster 6-and-5 record. Mizzou suffered some disappointing losses during the 1976 season, but still had one great upset to come – just two weeks later.

Missouri captains (left to right): Steve Pisarkiewicz, Tom Hodge, and Curtis Brown with Coach Al Onofrio.

"Nuts, nuts, nuts, nuts!"

Ohio State Head Coach Woody Hayes, shown here in his younger days, probably picked up a few gray hairs during his only meeting with Missouri. (Courtesy of The Ohio State University Department of Athletics)

Missouri 22 — Ohio State 21

Tiger Woods
SEPTEMBER 25, 1976

Missouri's startling string of upsets in the 1970s didn't begin or end with Pete Woods. But the Tiger quarterback from University City may have defined Missouri's decade of upsets.

Woods, in his first college start against Ohio State, ran for the deciding 2-point conversion with 12 seconds left in the game. He had propelled Missouri to another dramatic victory in one of college football's most hostile environments.

The Tigers had opened the season on the road with a 46-25 pasting of then eighth-ranked Southern Cal. But they turned right around the following week and lost at home, 31-6, to a so-so Illinois team. No one could be sure which Tiger team would show up.

One thing was certain. Mizzou quarterback Steve Pisarkiewicz, the man who directed the upset at USC, wouldn't show – at least not in uniform. The injured Pisarkiewicz watched from the sidelines in street clothes.

Woods wasn't expected to play at all that season. Tiger Coach Al Onofrio hoped to redshirt Woods while "Zark" ran the show. But Pisarkiewicz was on borrowed time. He had injured his right shoulder and hand before the USC game. He had to leave the Illinois debacle in the third quarter. Woods, who participated in only 10 plays prior to the Ohio State tilt, was pressed into service.

The odds against a successful starting debut by Woods were enormous. To say the Buckeyes were hard to beat at home would be like saying *The Beatles* had a few hit records. Woody Hayes' legions hadn't lost in Ohio Stadium in five years. The previous week they scored their 25th consecutive home victory, a 17-9 victory over seventh-ranked Penn State.

Missouri had never beaten the Buckeyes in their own backyard. In fact, the Tigers hadn't beaten Ohio State anywhere.

Ohio State was ranked second in the nation. The third-largest crowd in Ohio Stadium history – 87,936 – settled in to watch another Buckeye romp (with the exception, of course, of a smattering of Black and Gold faithful).

For the most part, the first half played according to form. Ohio State's mammoth fullback, 247-pound Pete Johnson, barreled his way through the Tiger defense for 103 yards and three touchdowns as Ohio State piled up a 21-7 halftime lead.

"He hit me so hard the first time that one of his Buckeye decals stuck on MY helmet," Tiger defensive tackle Curtis Kirkland told the *Columbia Missourian's* Davis Lundy.

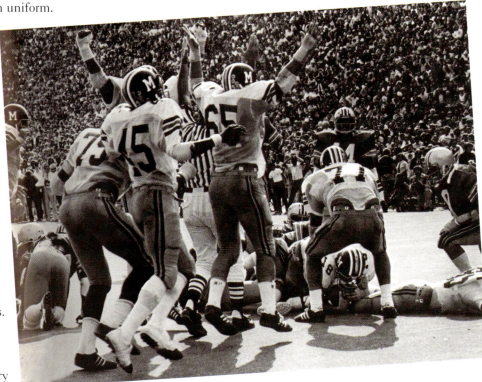

Pete Woods dives across the goal line for the winning 2-point conversion.

The Tigers did pull even, albeit briefly, in the second quarter. Wideout Joe Stewart outleaped a Buckeye defender to pull in a 31-yard touchdown pass from Woods.

Ohio State, behind Johnson, answered immediately with a 77-yard touchdown drive to go up 14-7.

On the Tigers' next possession, Ohio State All-American tackle Nick Buonamici, tipped and then intercepted a Woods' pass. That set up Johnson's third short TD run and a 14-point halftime edge.

Tiger linebacker Chris Garlich returned the favor in the third quarter. Garlich intercepted Rod Gerald's pass near midfield and returned the ball to the OSU 36-yard line. Garlich's interception set up a 4-yard touchdown run by Curtis Brown, trimming Ohio State's advantage to 21-14 with 8:54 left in the third quarter.

The Buckeye offense, so effective in the first half, continually spun its wheels against Missouri's defense in the second. Johnson rushed for only 19 yards in the final two quarters.

It all came down to the final five minutes of the game.

With 4:42 left to play, Missouri took possession on its own 20-yard line. In six plays the Tigers moved to the Ohio State 46 where disaster nearly struck.

Woods fumbled while attempting to pass. Brown recovered for an apparent loss of 13 yards. But, the Buckeyes were guilty of holding, the first of two major penalties in the closing minutes. Instead of second-and-23, Mizzou had a first-and-eight.

On third-and-six from the 40, Brown swept around right end, broke several tackles and sprinted 31 yards to the Ohio State 9-yard line.

A keeper by Woods gained 6 yards. Brown picked up another yard on second down.

With 16 seconds left, facing third-and-goal from the 2-yard line, the Tigers called their final timeout.

After the break, Woods took the snap, dropped back, and floated a pass for Leo Lewis in the far corner of the end zone. Lewis pulled in Woods' toss for the touchdown. Ohio State 21, Missouri 20. Twelve seconds remained.

Head Coach Al Onofrio, ignoring the old adage that you play for a win at home and a tie on the road,

never wavered in his decision: the Tigers would go for two and the win.

The noise level was incredible as Woods readied himself for the shotgun snap from center for the conversion try. Unable to hear, Woods stepped back and asked the officials for help. That only made it worse but the Tigers got some unexpected assistance from the Ohio State sidelines.

Irascible Woody Hayes, who had been extremely agitated during the Tigers' drive, walked out onto the field and asked for quiet.

After taking the snap, Woods rolled to his right and threw for Brown. The pass sailed just over Brown's outstretched fingers.

"I thought it was over," Woods said.

So did most of the crowd, including a group of Missourians huddled in the end zone seats. One Tiger fan, realizing a vocal retort would be futile, simply stood and pointed to a solitary piece of cloth which lay in the end zone – a referee's flag.

The Buckeyes were guilty of holding; Mizzou had another chance.

After an Ohio State timeout, Woods stood directly under center, the Tigers now a yard-and-a-half from pay dirt. Woods took the snap, rolled left on a sprint option, slipped a tackle, found a small opening and dived into the end zone. Mizzou 22, Ohio State 21.

Woods needed no help now from Hayes or the officials. With the exception of the small contingent of wildly ecstatic Tiger rooters, Ohio Stadium was silent.

Things weren't so quiet back in Columbia where another raucous celebration erupted, including one at the Hearnes Center, where nearly 800 fans had watched the game on a huge closed-circuit television screen. Hundreds poured out of bars, into the streets, and on to Faurot Field. This time the Columbia police force was prepared; the goalposts were saved.

Hayes' reaction was predictably volatile and terse. Perturbed by repeated questions about the penalty the Ohio State coach bellowed, "Nuts, nuts, nuts, nuts" and stormed out of the post-game press conference.

(Left) Tigers celebrate in Columbus.

(Below) Al Onofrio received the game ball after sending the Buckeyes to their first home loss in five years.

Joe Stewart (left) and Pete Woods

Missouri 34   Nebraska 24

"Woods Has The Goods"
OCTOBER 23, 1976

If there was ever one play that defined a Missouri football victory, it was Pete Woods' 98-yard touchdown pass to Joe Stewart in Mizzou's 34-24 victory over Nebraska in 1976. It's the story behind the play, and those involved in the play, that makes it one of the most memorable moments in Missouri football history.

The 1976 football season for the Tigers was bizarre to say the least. Mizzou scored upset victories on the road against eighth-ranked USC and second-ranked Ohio State, yet lost at home to pushovers like Illinois and Iowa State.

So, what did Mizzou fans expect when they traveled to Lincoln in late October for a road game against third-ranked Nebraska? An upset, what else.

Missouri was again the big underdog. The Tigers had to use backup quarterback Pete Woods because starting quarterback Steve Pisarkiewicz had an injured elbow. On the third play of the game, the Tigers lost starting running back Curtis Brown, the Big Eight's leading rusher, because of an injured back. Reserve Dean Leibson was pressed into action. But, Woods, Leibson, and of course, Joe Stewart played major roles in the upset victory.

Mizzou's offense moved the ball well in the first half. Woods hit Stewart on a 44-yard pass to Nebraska's 1-yard line. Two plays later, Woods scored to give Mizzou a 7-0 first quarter lead.

Nebraska responded with two touchdowns. The first score came when the Huskers blocked a Monte Montgomery punt and recovered the ball in the end zone. The second touchdown came on a Monte Anthony 1-yard run. Both extra-points failed and Nebraska led 12-7.

Mizzou answered with two more touchdowns before halftime. Woods completed a 9-yard scoring toss to tight end and future NFL Hall of Famer Kellen Winslow, his first career touchdown for Missouri. Woods later scored on a 1-yard run, and after Husker quarterback Vince Ferragamo answered with a 1-yard touchdown, Mizzou took a 23-18 lead to the locker room at halftime.

In the second half, Nebraska started to take control. The Cornhuskers scored six points on two field goals and led 24-23 after three quarters. With the Tigers facing the wind in the fourth quarter, and the Husker running game building momentum, Nebraska seemed confident of victory.

Early in the fourth quarter Missouri found itself backed up against its own goal at the 2-yard line. At this point the Tigers just wanted to grind out a couple of yards to give Montgomery a little more room to punt. After all, Montgomery already had one punt blocked earlier in the game for a Nebraska touchdown.

But, on third down and 14 yards to go, Mizzou went for broke. Woods called the play – "127 Ice Z Streak." Woods faked a handoff to Leibson at the line, took a short drop, and fired the ball to Stewart who caught the ball in stride on a streak pattern at the 35-yard line. Nebraska defensive back Dave Butterfield was fooled at the line of scrimmage and slipped. Stewart was all alone. Stewart, who was the fastest player on the Tiger squad, sprinted 98 yards for the longest touchdown from scrimmage in Big Eight Conference history.

To add insult to injury, Woods then passed to Stewart over Butterfield for the two-point conversion to give Mizzou a 31-24 lead with 12:53 to play in the game.

The Nebraska crowd was stunned, and so were the players. Mizzou added a Tim Gibbons field goal and came away with a 34-24 upset of third-ranked Nebraska at Lincoln.

After the game, the talk centered on the play – Woods' 98-yard touchdown pass to Stewart.

Nebraska Head Coach Tom Osborne: "It was a mix-up in coverage. There was a breakdown in communication. There were lots of turning points in games like this, but until that point we thought we had things pretty well under control."

Burned Husker defensive back Dave Butterfield: "The call in the huddle had me covering the flat, but since they were in a two tight end offense there was

(Far opposite right to left) Pete Woods fakes handoff to Dean Leibson. Woods fires pass to Stewart. Nebraska safety Larry Valasek dives in vain. Stewart completes the longest play from scrimmage in Big Eight history. (Courtesy Nebraska Husker Vision Archives)

(Below) "Woods Has The Goods"

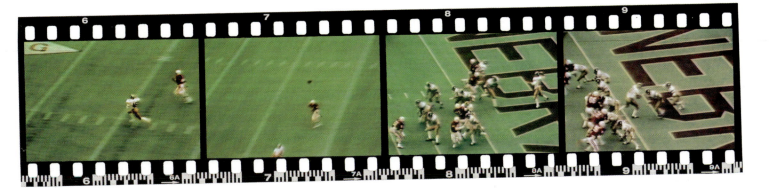

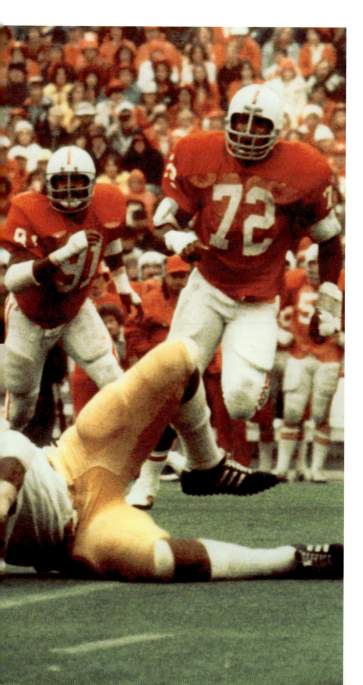

supposed to be a change where I'd take deep. But we just didn't get it communicated."

Missouri wide receiver Joe Stewart countered the mix-up in coverage theory by saying, "I could have beat him (Butterfield) anyway." Stewart put the play into perspective by telling reporters after the game, "It definitely was the turning point in the game. After that, when they got the ball, they weren't so confident."

And then Stewart made the understatement of the day, "I guess this was the best touchdown I ever scored."

No one would argue that point.

As the Nebraska fans sadly filed out of Memorial Stadium that day, two Missouri coeds who made the trip to Lincoln carried a sign across the field. It read: "Woods Has The Goods."

No one would argue that point either.

The Nebraska victory was the last big hurrah for the Tigers in their roller coaster 1976 season. They finished 6-and-5 with embarrassing home losses against Illinois, Iowa State and Kansas. But, the 1976 season will forever be remembered for the three stunning road upsets of eighth-ranked USC, second-ranked Ohio State, and third-ranked Nebraska.

M-I-Z! Z-O-U!

1976

As the Missouri state legislature recognized the Mizzou football team for its accomplishments during the 1998 season, the Tigers suddenly found themselves in the midst of an unusual spectacle at the State Capitol: a non-partisan, political rally.

"M-I-Z!" the Democrats shouted.

"Z-O-U!" the Republicans immediately responded.

And on it went.

Stand in any public gathering in the state of Missouri and yell, "M-I-Z!" and someone is sure to yell back, "Z-O-U!"

How did the most famous of all University of Missouri cheers begin? To answer that question, you have to go back to the 1976 football season.

On September 25, 1976, the Tigers pulled off a tremendous upset over second ranked Ohio State at Columbus, Ohio. Mizzou won 22-21 by scoring the winning touchdown and two-point conversion in the final seconds of the game.

During that game, Missouri cheerleaders were impressed with one Ohio State cheer in particular. The Ohio State cheerleaders induced their fans on opposite sides of the stadium to cheer back and forth. The crowd shouted, "O," then "HI," then "O," spelling out their state's name, "Ohio." The cheer went over and over again. Each side of the stadium appeared to be answering the other.

Mizzou cheerleader Jess Bushyhead recalled, "It was a rhythmically powerful cheer. We were speechless, having never thought of doing something like that before."

So, on the long bus ride back to Columbia, Bushyhead got together with fellow cheerleaders Jim Henry, Steve Wendling, Marty Handy, Dottie Bellman, Amy Lissner, Anne Pobanz, Laurie Flynn, Becky Kamitsuka, Bill Irwin and Greg Johnson, and asked the question, "What can we do to go the Buckeyes one better at home in Columbia?"

There were suggestions of one side of the stadium yelling, "M," and the other side responding, "U." One side could yell, "Black," the other side could yell, "Gold." According to Bushyhead, it was at that point in the conversation that Mini-Mizzou member Cedric Lemmie chimed in and said, "How about M-I-Z – Z-O-U?" The idea for a new cheer had been born, but now came the problem of how to implement it.

At the next home game on October 2, 1976, the Tigers hosted North Carolina at Faurot Field. During that game the band seated in the north end zone yelled, "M-I-Z," to the

1976 Missouri cheer squad started the famous "M-I-Z! Z-O-U!" echo.

Memorable Moments • 95

The Tiger card section gets involved.

cheerleaders who were in the south end zone. The cheerleaders with their megaphones and P.A. system yelled back, "Z-O-U." Back and forth it went, band to cheerleaders, end zone to end zone.

"I remember it going over a bit strangely primarily because the crowd didn't really know what we were doing or if they should participate," Bushyhead recalled. "So we decided to take the concept a step further."

So, at the next home football game at Faurot Field, on October 16, 1976, against Iowa State, the cheerleaders tried to get the crowd involved in this new "M-I-Z – Z-O-U" cheer. According to Bushyhead, here's what happened:

"The cheerleaders actually got up in the stands and told everyone seated opposite the band that when the band yelled, 'M-I-Z,' we would yell back, 'Z-O-U.' So just before kickoff, we tried it. The band yelled 'M-I-Z,' and to our astonishment, the crowd yelled back with us, 'Z-O-U.' Everyone was fired up about this cool new cheer we'd created. It was all we talked about during the first half, and how we could make it happen again, but even bigger with the entire crowd – not just end zone-to-end zone but side-to-side."

At halftime Bushyhead put his plan to work. He talked with fellow cheerleaders and enlisted the pompon girls to help. Bushyhead sent the cheerleaders into the stands with their megaphones and explained to the crowd what was going to happen.

Cheerleaders instructed fans, "Hey, did you hear that 'M-I-Z – Z-O-U' thing before kickoff? We want to do it again before the second half kickoff but with opposite sides of the stadium."

Bushyhead recalled, "We all knew it was going to work – you could feel it. Hundreds of people were asking us, 'When? When? When?' Just as the Tigers came back on to the field we split up into two groups, one on the west side the other on the east side, scattering ourselves in the crowd with megaphones. We had also synchronized our watches so we'd know pretty closely when to be listening for the first few yells from across the field."

Pompon girl Debbie Storehalder Danuser also remembered it well: "Jess said, 'We're going to try this. Pompons on one side, cheerleaders on the other. You're going to say 'M-I-Z' and then point to us on the other side of the stadium.' We'd say 'M-I-Z' and the crowd would say 'what are they saying?' and didn't respond at first. The crowd looked strangely at us."

Fellow pompon girl Dee Anne Tongate Gie (who married Mizzou kicker Anthony Gie) said, "The first few times we did it, it was flat. Only the lower levels could hear us. Gradually it caught on to the upper levels."

"It started," said Bushyhead. "Small at first, so lost in the sound of the crowd you almost couldn't hear it. But within a few cycles the crowd caught on. Within minutes it seemed to surpass in power, volume and enthusiasm the Ohio State version we'd derived it from."

The Golden Girls and Marching Mizzou

"It was wonderful," said Gie. "It carries the whole stadium away."

The "M-I-Z – Z-O-U" cheer continued to pick up steam for the rest of the 1976 football season. It was also used successfully during the 1976-77 basketball season. And, by the 1977 football season, any Tiger fan could yell out, "M-I-Z," and a response of, "Z-O-U," was sure to follow.

There was no master plan, no committee meetings that created the most famous cheer in the history of the University of Missouri. Just a bunch of creative and energetic college kids. Members of the cheerleading, pompon and Mini-Mizzou squads in 1976 conceived, improvised and implemented a cheer that will energize and unite Mizzou fans, students and alums for generations to come.

(Above) "M-I-Z! Z-O-U!" - the fan's favorite

(Left) The creators of "M-I-Z! Z-O-U!"

Memorable Moments • 99

Warren Powers leads the Tigers on the field for his first game as Missouri's head coach.

Missouri 3  Notre Dame 0

Powers Surge
SEPTEMBER 9, 1978

The Mizzou Tigers – with a new coach, new offense, and new defense – faced an old problem. They were massive underdogs in their season opener, on the road against one of the nation's elite football powers.

In two of the three previous seasons, Missouri took to the road in its opener and overhauled the nation's second-ranked team.

Dan Devine, coach of the defending national champion Irish, was well-versed in Missouri tradition. Devine coached the Tigers to many of their biggest wins and finest seasons as Missouri's head coach from 1958 to 1970.

But Devine eschewed the field goal against his old school, passing up almost sure 3-pointers on four occasions. On a 90-degree afternoon, Missouri's defense put Notre Dame in the deep freeze, stopping the Irish on four fourth down plays deep in Tiger territory.

"They came up with the big play all day on defense, and often on offense, too," Devine said. "I would also like to be critical of myself for not realizing that field goals win football games."

Warren Powers, making his debut as Missouri's head coach, had no trouble arriving at that conclusion. When Missouri faced a fourth-and-one at the Irish 16-yard line early in the fourth quarter, Powers didn't hesitate to send in freshman kicker Jeff Brockhaus.

"No, hell no I wasn't thinking of going for it," Powers said.

Brockhaus nailed the 33-yard field goal for the only points of the game.

The Tigers' defensive unit refused to wilt in the heat. In the first half Missouri's Chris Garlich and Eric Wright each intercepted Irish quarterback Joe Montana.

In the second half Notre Dame penetrated Missouri's 25-yard line five times. The Irish failed on fourth down tries from the 11, 1, 14 and 27 yard lines and fumbled away a fifth chance.

"We just beat them physically," Tiger defensive back Russ Calabrese said. "Our defense, especially our defensive line, was really in form that game. Our defensive line just handled 'em."

In the third quarter, when Notre Dame went for the first down on fourth-and-one from the 11, Mizzou stopped Montana's sneak attempt.

Later in the third quarter, Notre Dame had second-and-goal from the Missouri 2. Two running plays up the middle moved the Irish one yard closer. On fourth down, running back Vagas Ferguson tried to go outside. Garlich and Kurt Peterson nailed him for a 3-yard loss.

In the fourth quarter, Montana moved the Irish to the Missouri 27. On fourth-and-one Mizzou linebacker Billy Bess stacked up Irish fullback Jerome Heavens at the line of scrimmage.

On fourth-and-four from the

Russ Calabrese was a marked man at Notre Dame.

"I told him, 'Hey buddy, you helped me out.'"

After the botched Notre Dame field goal attempt, Missouri's new pro veer offense finally got untracked. Using screen passes to diffuse Notre Dame's pass rush, sophomore quarterback Phil Bradley directed Mizzou from its own 14 to the Irish 16.

That was close enough for Brockhaus' game-winner.

The Tigers still weren't out of the woods. Far from it.

In the closing minutes, Notre Dame advanced to the Missouri 25. But Tiger end Wendell Ray forced Jerome Heavens to fumble. Eric Berg recovered for Mizzou.

The Tigers failed to advance after the fumble recovery, setting the stage for another clutch play, this one by the their punter.

Missouri 14, Devine finally elected to kick. But Joe Restic fumbled the snap and threw an incomplete pass.

Notre Dame actually advanced to the Missouri 3-yard line on the drive, but only momentarily. Montana teamed with receiver Kris Haines on a 34-yard pass play. But, when Haines got up, he slapped the helmet of Calabrese, earning a personal foul penalty.

Calabrese had been an object of derision the entire game. In Columbia, he made some remarks to a student reporter in jest and off the record (he thought) that he grew up hating Notre Dame. His comments appeared in print and eventually ended up as "wallpaper" in the Notre Dame locker room.

"It was hostile with all the alumni on the sidelines," Calabrese recalled. "They were quite brutal and nasty to me the whole game. I also remember it was about 110 (degrees) on the field and they didn't even have ice for us in the first half."

Calabrese said Haines apologized for the head slap.

(Top left and middle) Missouri stopped the Irish four times deep in Tiger territory. (Bottom right) Freshman kicker Jeff Brockhaus scored the game's only points.

Monte Montgomery had struggled all day. His previous six punts, which included a partial block and a shank, netted only 131 yards, a 21.8 average.

"I wanted to kick myself in the ass after those horrible punts," Montgomery told the *Columbia Daily Tribune*. "But I probably would have missed it."

Montgomery's next punt was dead solid perfect. The booming spiral traveled 55 yards. When Irish punt returner Randy Harrison fumbled the kick, Norman Goodman recovered for Mizzou to wipe out Notre Dame's final hope.

The loss was Notre Dame's first in 11 games and the first time the Irish were blanked at home since 1960.

"It's great, great," Powers exuded after the game. "I can't say enough about our defense. They played inspired defense out there."

In post-upset tradition, students back in Columbia, took to the streets and then zeroed in on Faurot Field.

"Goal posts, goal posts, goal posts," echoed their chant.

The fans succeeded in climbing the fences to enter the field but the Columbia Police pitched another shutout that day. The goal posts remained standing.

(Above) Mizzou punter Monte Montgomery wanted to kick himself until the final moments.

(Below) Dan Devine coached Missouri to many great wins but suffered this loss to his old team.

Nebraska defenders got tired of tackling James Wilder.

Missouri 35   Nebraska 31

Running Wild(er)
NOVEMBER 18, 1978

As fate would have it, the schedule maker played a big part in giving Mizzou an exciting, nostalgic, sentimental, revengeful, and upsetting finish to the 1978 regular season. For the only time in Missouri football history, the Tigers final regular season game was against Nebraska.

And, as fate would have it, Missouri was led by first-year head coach Warren Powers who played football and was an assistant coach for eight seasons at Nebraska. If Powers could beat his alma mater, Missouri would earn its first bowl game in five years.

The schedule maker set up the possibility of an exciting finish, but it was up to the Tigers to make it happen. And in particular, two Mizzou players who would later star in the NFL, played their greatest games in a Tiger uniform on a day where the wind chill was near zero at Memorial Stadium in Lincoln, Nebraska. Those two players: James Wilder and Kellen Winslow.

Running back James Wilder played 11 seasons in the NFL for Tampa Bay, Washington and Detroit. Tight end Kellen Winslow played 10 seasons for the San Diego Chargers in a career that culminated with his induction into the Pro Football Hall of Fame in Canton, Ohio. Even though he was only a sophomore, Wilder demonstrated to scouts the type of power running back he would become in the NFL. Winslow gave the football world a look at the prototype NFL tight end of the future.

The 1978 game against Nebraska did not start the way Mizzou wanted. The Cornhuskers scored on the first play from scrimmage when running back Rick Berns bolted around left end for 82-yards, a touchdown and a 7-0 Nebraska lead. Berns had the game of his career, rushing for 255 yards on 36 carries against the Tiger defense.

Mizzou came right back, going 79 yards on the running of Wilder, Earl Gant and Gerry Ellis. Wilder scored from nine yards out on a run up the middle to tie the game 7-7.

Next time the Cornhuskers had the ball, they scored. Once again, it was Berns slashing through the Tiger defense for most of the yards on the touchdown drive. The Huskers later added a field goal and led 17-7.

But, the Tigers had too many offensive weapons to fold. Wilder started running – wildly. He ran over and through tacklers

Tiger quarterback Phil Bradley guided the Tiger offense.

Memorable Moments • 105

Tight end Kellen Winslow had his best game as a Tiger.

for 38 yards on a touchdown drive that finished with quarterback Phil Bradley passing to Winslow for a 14-yard touchdown. Mizzou trailed 17-14 at the half.

The second half began the same way as the first half, with Berns ripping through the Missouri defense. He carried the ball on eight of the 13 plays in a 72-yard drive that culminated with his 2-yard touchdown to give Nebraska a 24-14 lead. But, the Tigers did not fold.

"When the defense let up, the offense picked them up," Powers told reporters after the game.

Wilder and Winslow once again provided the offensive lift. On the next drive, Winslow caught two passes and Wilder continued his collision course with the Nebraska defense. Wilder finished off the drive with his second touchdown of the game, a 1-yard run to pull the Tigers within three points of the Huskers.

On the next Nebraska drive the Tigers finally got the big defensive play they needed. Nebraska quarterback Tom Sorley passed over the middle to Kenny Brown, but Mizzou linebacker Chris Garlich stepped in front to make the interception and the Tigers had the ball at the Nebraska 31-yard line.

After Phil Bradley scrambled for 27 yards to the 4-yard line, Wilder crashed over for his third touchdown of the game. The Tigers led for the first time, 28-24.

But the Cornhuskers responded. They went back to the ground attack. Berns carried the load on the Huskers 89-yard 15-play drive that put Nebraska

ahead 31-28 at the end of the third quarter. That set the stage for the dramatic fourth quarter and the heroics of Wilder, Winslow and Garlich.

The Tigers actually had two chances to take the lead in the fourth quarter. Bradley passed 35 yards to Leo Lewis who took the ball to the Nebraska 4-yard line. But, three plays later, Gant fumbled and Nebraska recovered.

Mizzou's defense then tightened and stopped Nebraska, setting up one final drive for the Tigers to win the game.

With 5:59 left in the game, Missouri began its drive from its own 26-yard line, and once again the stars were Wilder and Winslow. Wilder carried the load on the ground, and Winslow made the key reception of the drive, a 33-yard catch from Bradley.

On the seventh play of the drive, on a 7-yard run, Wilder scored his fourth touchdown of the game to give Mizzou a 35-31 lead. For those who saw it, it was the most spectacular 7-yard run in Missouri football history. Wilder literally bowled over and through the Nebraska defense, decking several defenders on his way to the end zone. One writer wrote that day that it looked as if the Nebraska defenders were getting tired of tackling Wilder.

Mizzou couldn't celebrate for long, because Nebraska still had time to score. With two minutes to play, somebody finally stopped Nebraska's Rick Berns. It was Garlich. On third-and-three, Garlich, with his 21st tackle of the game, stopped Berns cold.

"My head hurts and I feel like throwing up," Garlich told reporters after the game.

Linebacker Chris Garlich made 21 tackles against the Cornhuskers.

On fourth down, Sorley's pass fell incomplete and the Tigers held on for a 35-31 upset victory over second-ranked Nebraska.

"I can't believe they beat us," Berns said after the game.

Believe it. Tom Osborne did.

"Missouri just beat us. We had trouble stopping them on offense," the Nebraska coach told reporters after the game. "I'd say the two major reasons we lost were that we did not control the line of scrimmage on defense and we were not tackling like we should have."

No doubt that was in reference to the spectacular game of Wilder, who carried the ball 28 times for 181 yards, four touchdowns, and countless broken tackles.

"You just get cranked up. This is terrific. It feels good, man. It feels good," Wilder said after the game.

Winslow called the game the greatest of his college career. Winslow made six catches for 132 yards and one touchdown.

The loss knocked the second-ranked Huskers out of a chance for a national championship showdown against Penn State. Nebraska wound up in the Orange Bowl against Oklahoma.

With the win, the Tiger players voted to accept a bid to the Liberty Bowl where they would beat LSU 20-15 and finish the season ranked 15th in the *Associated Press* poll.

And, for Head Coach Warren Powers, his first regular season at Mizzou began with an upset over fifth-ranked Notre Dame, and finished with an upset over his alma mater Nebraska.

"I don't think I could be happier right now. It was one great football game. Our kids played their hearts out," he said.

Tiger guard Mark Jones celebrates Wilder's winning touchdown.

The 1983 Holiday Bowl program cover (Courtesy Holiday Bowl)

Missouri 17 — BYU 21

The Flea-FLICKER
HOLIDAY BOWL - DECEMBER 23, 1983

Missouri's football history is one of heroic performances, spectacular finishes, and great upsets. It's also a history of heartbreaking losses in the most unusual ways. Case in point – the 1983 Holiday Bowl in San Diego against Brigham Young University.

The Tigers lost to one of the most prolific quarterbacks in college and NFL history, Steve Young. But, it wasn't a Steve Young touchdown pass that beat the Tigers; it was a Steve Young touchdown *reception* in the closing seconds that did in Mizzou.

Ninth-ranked BYU led the nation in total offense with nearly 600 yards per game. Missouri featured a stingy defense led by Bobby Bell, and for most of the game, Missouri's defense held the dynamic Cougar offense in check. The Tigers yielded 370 yards in offense, far below the BYU average.

During the regular season, Young threw only 10 interceptions in 429 attempts, yet the Tigers picked off Young three times. Still, Mizzou had numerous chances to win this game, but did not take advantage of the BYU mistakes and made plenty of their own.

Mizzou started the scoring in the first quarter on Eric Drain's 2-yard run. Drain was the offensive star of the game for the Tigers with 115 yards rushing.

BYU answered in the second quarter. Young scored on a 10-yard run to tie the game 7-7.

Defensive MVP Bobby Bell sacked BYU quarterback Steve Young four times.

Eric Drain led all rushers with 115 yards.

Still in the second quarter, Reco Hawkins intercepted Young at the BYU 29-yard line. But, the Tigers couldn't punch it into the end zone and settled for a Brad Burditt field goal and a 10-7 halftime lead.

The seesaw contest continued in the second half. After Missouri blocked a field goal attempt, the Tigers gave the ball back to the Cougars on a Jon Redd fumble. On the next play BYU regained the lead on a 33-yard touchdown pass from Young to Eddie Stinnett. Stinnett scored this touchdown with his hands and legs. Later, his arm would come into play.

Trailing 14-10, backup quarterback Warren Seitz led the Tigers on an impressive 80-yard drive to begin the fourth quarter. Seitz had taken the place of starting quarterback Marlon Adler, who sprained his ankle in the third quarter. Drain finished the nine-play drive with a 2-yard run, his second touchdown of the game, to give Missouri a 17-14 lead.

The Tigers had a chance to put the game out of reach late in the game. They drove the ball to the BYU 7-yard line.

On fourth-and-one, the Tigers handed the ball to Drain who was stopped near the first down marker. The officials spotted the ball and then picked up the ball and re-spotted it – to the detriment of the Tigers. When the Missouri coaches asked for an explanation of the re-spot, the officials said a player accidentally touched the ball and moved it slightly. The new spot came up short of the first down. Young and BYU had the ball with 93 yards to go and 3:57 left on the clock.

On the second play of the drive, Bell sacked Young for the fourth time in the game and Mizzou was looking good. On the next play, the Tiger defense once again flushed Young out of the pocket. He scrambled, and as he headed toward the sideline he heaved a desperation pass in the direction of Mike Eddo. It was a high, floating, wobbling pass that Eddo said looked like a punt. He caught it and

Brigham Young had the ball at the Missouri 36-yard line.

The Tiger defense tightened. Young was sacked for a nine-yard loss and BYU faced a fourth-and-ten with 37 seconds to play. Young flared the ball out to running back Waymon Hamilton near the sideline who caught it and made the first down by the narrowest of margins.

That set up the game winning play. With 31 seconds left, BYU had the ball at the 14-yard line. Young handed the ball off to Stinnett who started a sweep to the right side. He stopped, planted, and threw the ball back to Young who had slipped out of the backfield to the left flat. Young caught the ball over the outstretched arms of Bell, broke away from would-be tacklers, and dove into the end zone for the winning touchdown with 23 seconds left in the game. BYU won 21-17.

The irony of how the winning touchdown was scored was not lost on Young during post-game interviews.

"I throw for five million yards and I end my career catching the ball," he told reporters. "I didn't want to drop it because if I did they would bring me back and hang me from the top of the Brigham Young statue!"

Young won the game with his hands and feet. Stinnett, the running back, won it with his arm.

"I was shocked when I heard the call," Stinnett told Mike Smith of the *St. Louis Post-Dispatch*. "I was scared. There were only a couple of seconds left and I'd never thrown the thing in a game before."

The Tiger defense held Young to 314 yards passing on 24 completions, well below his average. Still, Young drew high praise from Mizzou Coach Warren Powers in a post-game tribute.

"I think Steve Young is the best quarterback I've ever seen in college football," Powers said.

Missouri fans got a close-up look at the final college game of one of the greatest quarterbacks in college and NFL history. They also saw a rarity: Steve Young beat Mizzou by catching the ball, not passing it.

In the end Steve Young (8) beat the Tigers catching the ball, rather than passing it (Courtesy Holiday Bowl).

The 1986 Missouri vs. Kansas program cover

Missouri 48   Kansas 0

Turnaround is Fair Play
NOVEMBER 22, 1986

Normally, a victory in a three-win season over an unranked opponent – even an arch rival – is no cause for mass celebration. But the victory-hungry Tiger Fans had just witnessed the biggest one-game turnaround in school history - an almost inconceivable 125-point swing.

The Faurot Field goal posts – off the endangered list over the last few seasons – met their demise shortly after the 48-0 romp over Kansas became official.

"I'm on top of the world right now," said offensive tackle John Clay, one of 16 Tiger seniors who had just played their last home game.

Just two weeks earlier the Tigers had suffered their worst loss ever, a 77-0 shellacking at Oklahoma.

More important than the point reversal was the 180-degree swing in emotion. The Tigers fell to 2-7 on the season after the Oklahoma humiliation. An open week on the schedule gave them time to mend their physical and psychological wounds.

The extra week also allowed the "Dump Woody" sentiment to fester. Head Coach Woody Widenhofer, a former Mizzou player, had won only three of his first 20 games since inheriting the head coaching job from Warren Powers in 1985.

Realizing losses to KU were the death knells for Powers and his predecessor Al Onofrio, Widenhofer announced to the Columbia Quarterback Club, "I'll tell you right now, we'll beat Kansas."

Prior to the Kansas game Widenhofer allowed the Tigers to open up their pre-game music selection. Just before kickoff the Mizzou locker room bellowed with sounds of *The Beasty Boys*.

"They let us kick the box in," running back Darrel Wallace said. "Everybody got excited and pumped up."

Widenhofer believed the team's performance had more to do with the fact that his players were rested and healthy. Regardless, the beasty Tigers got their "bodies movin'" against the Jayhawks.

Mizzou racked up 488 yards of total offense. Twelve different Tigers rushed for a combined 358 yards, led by Wallace's 106 yards on 28 carries.

Missouri's defense – the third-worst scoring defense in the nation, a unit that yielded 681 rushing yards at Oklahoma – limited Kansas to 55 yards rushing. The Tigers also registered the schools' first shutout in three

Woody Widenhofer guarantees a win over Kansas at the Columbia Quarterback Club (file photo courtesy Columbia Missourian).

Vernon Boyd congratulates Darrell Wallace, who led the Tigers with 106 yards rushing.

years (ironically, a 10-0 blanking of Oklahoma in 1983).

The Tigers scored methodically and they scored explosively.

Their first touchdown, a 2-yard run by quarterback Ronnie Cameron, capped a 10-play, 69-yard drive early in the first quarter. Their second touchdown, a 7-yard scramble by Cameron, ended a 14-run, 80-yard drive with only 1:29 left in the first half.

Counting Cameron's second touchdown, the Tigers scored 21 points in last 87 seconds of the first half. They quickly converted two Kansas turnovers into a pair of touchdown passes from Cameron to Victor Moore.

The first Cameron-to-Moore hookup covered 45 yards with 52 seconds left in the half. The next, a 35-yarder after Erik McMillan's interception, reached the end zone with only two seconds to go. The 29 points in 87 seconds increased Missouri's lead to 31-0 at intermission. The Tigers coasted from there.

As the final seconds ticked in the 48-0 victory, players hoisted Widenhofer to their shoulders, but only for a moment.

"I told them to put me down," Widenhofer said. "I'm not real excited about being carried off the field with three victories."

Mizzou fans weren't so willing to low-key this wing-ding. Starved for a victory celebration, they stormed the field and circled the goal posts.

Campus police put up some initial resistance but, in the end, were no more successful protecting the goal posts than Kansas had been protecting the goal line.

(Above) Missouri scored 21 points in 87 seconds including Ronnie Cameron's two touchdown passes to Victor Moore (Courtesy Mizzou Sports Properties/KOMU).

(Below) It's "party time" for the victory-hungry Tiger fans.

Memorable Moments • 115

The touchdown signal on Colorado's Fifth Down drew the ire of Tiger fans and players alike (Courtesy Fox Sports Net).

Missouri 31 Colorado 33

Fifth Down
OCTOBER 6, 1990

It is one of college football's most historic games.

It is Missouri's most infamous game – the 1990 "fifth down" game against Colorado at Faurot Field.

Missouri was looking for its second straight upset. The week before, the Tigers beat 21st-ranked Arizona State, 30-9. The 12th-ranked Buffaloes came to Columbia for the Big Eight opener for both teams.

The Tigers and the Buffaloes battled back and forth for the first 56 minutes of the game. A typical seesaw contest, Mizzou did most of its damage with an effective passing game, and Colorado gained its yards on the ground with its option attack. With 3:41 to play in the game, Colorado's Jim Harper broke a 24-24 tie with a 39-yard field goal to give the Buffaloes a 27-24 lead.

Mizzou responded, perhaps too quickly. The Tigers drove 80 yards in just four plays. They scored on Kent Kiefer's 38-yard touchdown pass to Damon Mays to take a 31-27 lead. One problem for the Tigers – they used only 1:09 on the clock. That gave Colorado 2:32 to mount one last drive.

The Buffaloes started their final drive from their own 12-yard line. They methodically moved downfield mixing the run and pass with several key plays. On second-and-four at the Missouri 9-yard line, Colorado quarterback Charles Johnson passed to tight end Jon Bowman. He slipped and went down near the sideline at the 3-yard line with 31 seconds to play. It was a Colorado first down, but because Bowman did not get out of bounds, the clock re-started when the chains were set.

So, on first down, Johnson spiked the football to stop the clock. Twenty-eight seconds remained.

On second down from the 3-yard line, Colorado running back Eric Bienemy ran up the middle but was stopped at the 1-yard line. Colorado called its last timeout with 18 seconds remaining. It was at this point when the officials

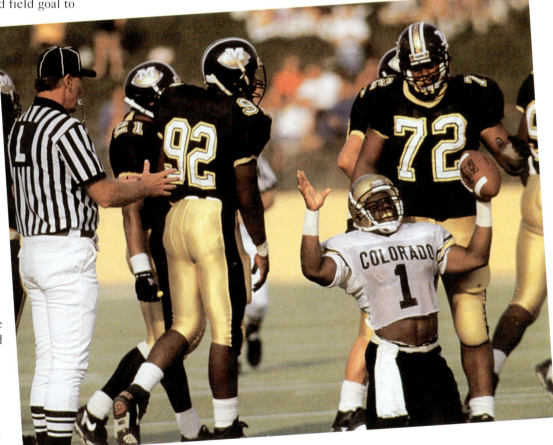

Eric Bienemy "slipped" his way to 225 yards rushing.

Memorable Moments • 117

Missouri Head Coach Bob Stull

From left to right, the fifth down...

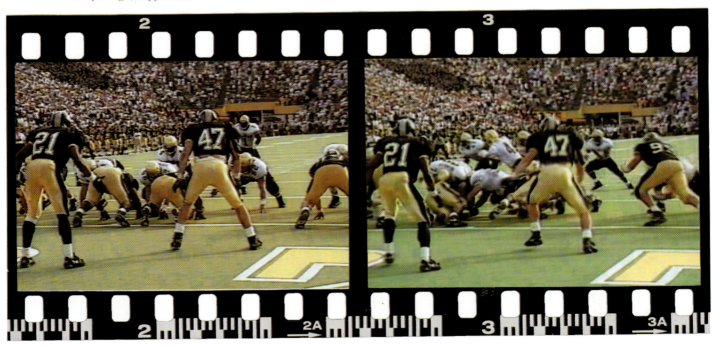

118 • MizzouRah!

failed to flip the down-marker. The down-marker remained on second down instead of being advanced to third down.

So, on third down (but the down-marker showed second down) Bienemy ran up the middle again, but was viciously thrown back by Mizzou defenders Tom Reiner, Mike Ringgenberg and Maurice Benson. Time was running. The officials stopped the clock at eight seconds to clear the pile. The officials then re-started the clock and time was running down.

So, on fourth down (but the down-marker showed third down) and with no timeouts, Johnson spiked the ball to stop the clock. Game over? Well, the officials didn't think so. They looked at the down-marker and said the Buffaloes had one more play. Missouri Head Coach Bob Stull said an assistant coach, a sideline reporter and backup quarterback Phil Johnson were the only people on the Missouri sideline who said, "That was fourth down."

"There was no confusion, no discussion on the field among officials or the chain crew that there was a problem with the down situation, so we didn't call a timeout. We didn't want to give Colorado extra time to call a play," Stull recalled. "The scoreboard said it was fourth down. The down-marker said it was fourth down. We were just trying to come up with a defense to stop Colorado on what we thought was fourth down."

So, with two seconds on the clock, and on fifth down (but the down-marker showed fourth down) Johnson ran the ball around right end. Tiger defenders hit him before the goal line and thought they had stopped him.

Television replays showed Johnson hit the turf on his buttock before the goal line, and then bounced and reached with the ball toward the goal line. At first, no officials signaled touchdown. But the official on the goal nearest to Johnson delayed his call before running toward Johnson with his arms up signaling a touchdown. No time on the clock. Scoreboard: Colorado 33, Missouri 31.

Students poured on the field. They started tearing down the goalpost in the south end zone. Mayhem on the field. Students and fans got in the officials' faces protesting the call. Missouri coaches and players pleaded their case that they stopped Johnson short.

Both teams headed for the locker room, and then came back on the field for the extra-point. Colorado didn't even try the point-after. They snapped the ball and downed it. Now the game was over, but the talking, protesting, rationalizing and damage control was just beginning.

When did Mizzou's coaching staff realize that Colorado had an extra down?

"Well after the game. At least a half hour, maybe an hour," Stull said.

When it sunk in that his team lost on a fifth

...Is Charles Johnson in?...

...continued on the next page...

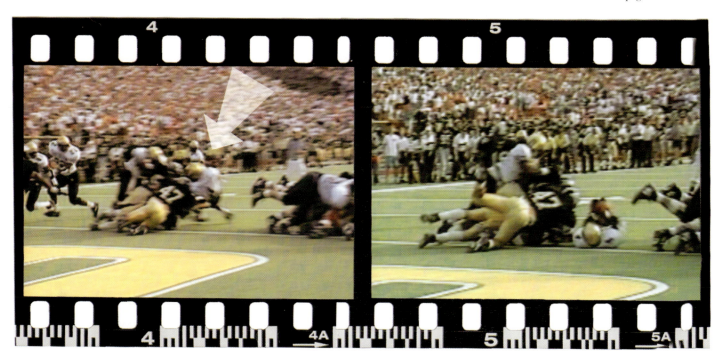

down, Stull remembered how he felt: "I got hacked off. It makes you ill. I kept saying to myself, 'How in the world could this happen?' We were amazed that it wasn't caught. Nobody thinks about it (an extra down)."

Mizzou defensive tackle Mario Johnson told reporters after the game, "They need to reverse that. I don't see how you can keep it that way. That's giving the game away. How can you give somebody five downs? That's a penalty. You cannot do that."

Mizzou safety Harry Colon on whether Charles Johnson scored on fifth down: "In my opinion he didn't get in. He hit the ground first and then hit the side of the goal line. He grabbed the ball, fumbled it for a second and then put it over his head."

Colorado Head Coach Bill McCartney changed the topic from the fifth down to the Omniturf playing surface at Faurot Field.

"The biggest story here is not the way the game ended. The biggest story is that field is not playable. No one should have to come in here and play on that surface. I'd rather play in a parking lot," McCartney told reporters after the game.

McCartney said Missouri failed to water the field, which made it even more slippery. He added that his team's option attack was hampered by the slick Omniturf, yet the Buffaloes rushed for a whopping 357 yards. Star Colorado running back Eric Bienemy "slipped" his way to 225 yards rushing in the game.

Reporters then asked McCartney if he felt Colorado stole the game.

"No, I don't feel like we stole one. I feel if our kids could have stood up we would have had a couple more scores," he rationalized.

"Both teams were playing on the same field," retorted Missouri offensive coordinator Dirk Koetter.

And then there's the question of the officials and their final ruling. Harassed by fans on the field, the officials raced to their dressing room, which was heavily guarded by police. Head linesman J.C. Louderback announced the officials would stand by their call, that Colorado was allotted only four downs in the final sequence of events.

Umpire Frank Gaines added, "If we screwed this up, nobody's going away

...Johnson scores on the fifth down - or did he? (Courtesy Mizzou Sports Properties/KOMU)

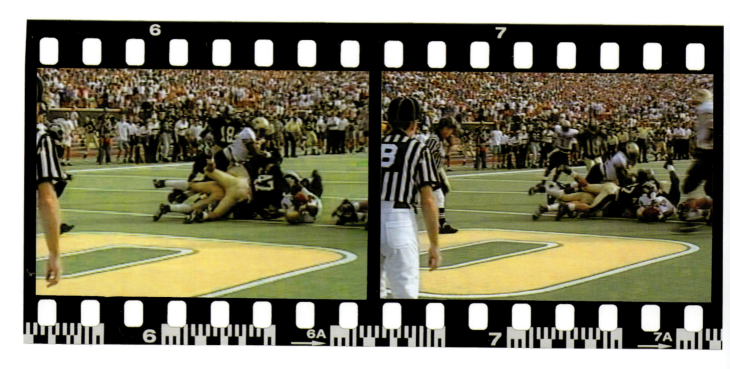

Mizzou fans prepare to storm the field.

from here feeling any worse than we are."

The 46,000 Missouri fans at Faurot Field that day would beg to differ. They, and all college football fans (including Colorado Buffalo fans), now know that the officials did screw it up.

After the Colorado game, Missouri stumbled through yet another disappointing season, finishing 4-and-7.

Colorado went on to win the national championship in a season where they beat a team on a fifth down on the final play of the game – a play that should never have been allowed to happen. Because of that, Colorado's national championship will forever be a tainted one in the minds of Mizzou football fans everywhere.

The official play-by-play sheet clearly shows Colorado scored on FIFTH down.

1-G, MU 3 — Charles Johnson pass incomplete

2-G, MU 3 — Eric Bienemy runs middle, gain of 2 (Reiner)

3-G, MU 1 — Bienemy runs middle, no gain (Reiner, Benson)

4-G, MU 1 — Johnson pass incomplete

5-G, MU 1 — Johnson runs middle, TOUCHDOWN

(Johnson runs for PAT, no good)

Memorable Moments • 121

Corby Jones tossed the tying pass and scored the winning touchdown.

Missouri 51 — Oklahoma State 50
2 OVERTIMES

Stilled Hearts at Stillwater
OCTOBER 25, 1997

The 1997 season gave Missouri its first good chance to have a winning season since 1983. The Tigers entered their game against 12th-ranked Oklahoma State at Stillwater with a 4-and-3 record, and Mizzou was coming off an impressive 37-29 win over Texas the week before.

The Tigers knew a win over undefeated Oklahoma State could propel them to their first bowl game since the 1983 Holiday Bowl against Brigham Young. A loss could lead them to their 14th losing season in a row. Yes – the Oklahoma State game would be the turning point of the season.

Mizzou surprised the Cowboys in the first half. After falling behind 7-0, the Tigers rolled off 30 straight points. Missouri quarterback Corby Jones led the way with three touchdown passes in the first half to give the Tigers a 30-7 lead. Missouri's ground attack was also in high gear, grinding out 221 yards in the game against a Cowboy defense that held five of six previous opponents to less than 100 yards on the ground. Mizzou was in complete control of the game, but that would change after intermission.

Oklahoma State came out in the second half and did to Mizzou what the Tigers had done to them in the first half – dominate and score 30 straight points. Momentum turned quickly and ferociously.

"I don't think we lost our poise," Missouri Head Coach Larry Smith told reporters after the game. "I just think they were making plays and we weren't."

The Tigers may not have lost their poise, but they did lose their lead. When Oklahoma State quarterback Tony Lindsay passed to tight end Alonzo Mayes for a 9-yard touchdown with just under two minutes left in the fourth quarter, the Cowboys took a 37-30 lead.

Seldom-used Ricky Ross loomed large for the Tigers.

Memorable Moments · 123

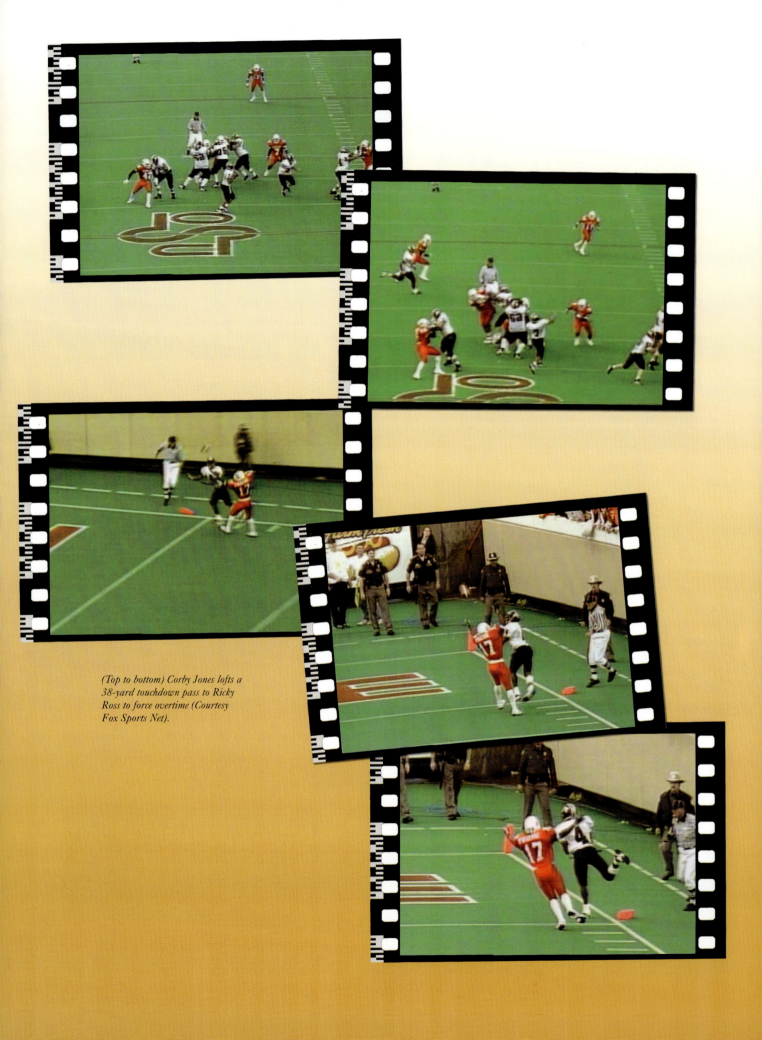

(Top to bottom) Corby Jones lofts a 38-yard touchdown pass to Ricky Ross to force overtime (Courtesy Fox Sports Net).

Could the Tigers come back with one final drive in the final two minutes after blowing a 23-point second half lead? That question was answered by Corby Jones and wide receiver Ricky Ross.

Mizzou's final drive began at its own 20-yard line with 1:57 left in the fourth quarter. The Tigers' offense was stuck in reverse. On their first three plays they lost two yards. So, on fourth-and-12, with the season on the line, Jones looked for Ross, a seldom-used wide receiver who had been suspended earlier in the season for violating team rules.

Ross hauled in an 18-yard pass across the middle to keep the drive alive. Four plays later the duo would hook up again on one of the most memorable touchdown passes in Missouri football history.

With 26 seconds left, the Tigers went for broke. They sent Ross on a streak pattern down the right sideline against Oklahoma State defensive back R.W. McQuarters. It was the match-up the Tigers were looking for.

"I told him in the huddle that I was going to be there," Ross told reporters after the game about his conversation with Jones.

Jones said he winked at Ross and told his wide receiver, "This one is coming to you."

At the snap, Ross sprinted straight down the sideline. Jones looked for no other receiver. McQuarters battled Ross all the way. The ball was right on target and Ross caught it in the corner of the end zone for a 38-yard touchdown with 18 seconds left in the fourth quarter. The extra-point was good and the Tigers tied the game, 37-37, and forced overtime.

Mizzou won the overtime coin flip and elected to go on defense. Oklahoma State scored on a Tony Lindsay touchdown pass and made the extra-point to take a 44-37 lead. The Tigers answered by scoring on a short Brock Olivo run, made the extra-point, and tied the game 44-44.

In the second overtime period, Mizzou had first possession. On the fourth play, Jones scored his second touchdown of the game on a 15-yard run. Extra-point was good and Mizzou led 51-44.

Now Oklahoma State got the ball for its possession in the second overtime period. Lindsay scored on a 6-yard run to pull Oklahoma State to within one point at 51-50.

Cowboys Coach Bob Simmons felt he'd had enough. Forget going for the tie. This game had been exhausting. Simmons and the Cowboys elected to go for the two-point conversion and the win.

Lindsay lined up in a bizarre formation. From the shotgun he had four offensive linemen in front of him. All the other players, backs and receivers, lined up to the left of the group of four linemen – first a group of two players, and split even farther a group of four players.

The Tigers weren't fooled. Lindsay dropped back to pass, but Mizzou defensive end Marquis Gibson forced Lindsay to scramble. As Lindsay started running toward the goal line, he was gang tackled at the 2-yard line. Missouri prevailed and won 51-50. The Stillwater crowd was silenced as they had just watched their Cowboys lose their first game of the season.

"I've never been involved in a game like this before," Tiger linebacker Barry Odom told reporters after the game. Who had?

So the Tigers won the turning-point game of their season. By knocking off previously unbeaten Oklahoma State, Missouri now had the look of a winner and a 5-and-3 record to show for it.

"I don't think I've ever been in a game with more emotional highs and lows than this, at least not any that I can think of," Missouri Head Coach Larry Smith said at his post-game news conference.

Just wait, Larry. Two weeks later, Smith and the Tigers would be part of a game that would surpass their double overtime win against Oklahoma State for emotional highs and lows, and with one of the craziest, most bizarre endings in college football history – the 1997 Nebraska game at Faurot Field.

Mizzou Coach Larry Smith and wife Cheryl were emotionally spent after the double-overtime victory.

Head Coach Larry Smith: "One stinkin' play!"

Missouri 38  Nebraska 45
IN OVERTIME
The Flea-KICKER
NOVEMBER 8, 1997

"One stinkin' play!"

That's how Missouri Head Coach Larry Smith summed up Missouri's loss to No. 1 ranked Nebraska in 1997. One stinkin' play separated Missouri, a football program known for huge upsets, from pulling off the greatest upset in Tiger football history.

Entering the 1997 game against Nebraska, Tiger fans sensed something special just might happen. Missouri hadn't beaten Nebraska in football since 1978, and hadn't won at Faurot Field against the Huskers since 1973. But, Missouri was enjoying its finest football season in 14 years. The Tigers were 6-and-3 and riding a three game winning streak with consecutive upset wins over Texas, Oklahoma State and Colorado.

Still, this was Nebraska. The top-ranked Cornhuskers in a powerhouse year. Missouri was a 29-point underdog.

An overflow crowd of almost 67,000 packed Faurot Field. Nebraska brought its usual strong contingent of 15,000 fans. They saw a game that went back and forth with neither team building more than a seven-point lead. They saw the only team that was able to go toe-to-toe with Nebraska all season long – the Missouri Tigers.

Missouri struck first on a short Brock Olivo touchdown run that capped a 78-yard drive. Corby Jones mixed the run and the pass brilliantly. The Tigers scored two more first half touchdowns on an 18-yard pass from Jones to Torey Coleman and a 34-yard pass from Jones to Olivo. Olivo made some nifty moves on his way to the end zone to give the Tigers a 24-21 halftime lead.

The second half produced more of the same as Nebraska battled back. The Cornhuskers rushed for 353 yards in the game. Ahman Green ran for 189 yards and Husker quarterback Scott Frost rushed for 141 yards. Frost scored from a yard out with three minutes left in the third quarter to give Nebraska a 28-24 lead.

But, the Tigers roared back. Devin West returned the ensuing kickoff 62 yards. Corby Jones later scored from six yards out and the Tigers went back on top 31-28 at the end of the third quarter.

The crowd at Faurot Field sensed an incredible fourth quarter to come. Nebraska Coach Tom Osborne called the atmosphere "supercharged" and said it reminded him of the Missouri/Nebraska battles during the mid-to-late 1970's. One thing was for certain; Missouri's football program hadn't seen this kind of enthusiasm, intensity and excitement for almost a generation.

Early in the fourth quarter Nebraska mounted a drive and settled for a field goal that tied the game at 31. Missouri responded. After a Harold Piersey interception that gave Mizzou the ball at the Nebraska 30-yard line, the Tigers went back on top when Jones completed a 15-yard touchdown pass to Eddie Brooks in the end zone. Missouri led 38-31 with 4:38 left in the fourth quarter. The Faurot Field crowd was delirious.

The Tigers' defense stopped the Huskers on their next possession. Missouri now had command of the ball and tried to run out the clock. With just 1:20 to play, Missouri faced a third-and-three situation on its own 47-yard line. Nebraska had one timeout left.

If Mizzou could get a first down, the Tigers would be able to run out the clock. But, Nebraska's defense stopped Jones on the option and forced Missouri to punt. A poor punt gave Nebraska the ball at its own 33-yard line with 1:02 left in the fourth quarter.

With 67 yards to go for a tying touchdown and a minute to play, Nebraska was forced to abandon its powerful rushing attack and go to the passing game, something the Huskers were not accustomed to, nor particularly adept at. That's when Scott Frost, the running quarterback, became Scott Frost the passing quarterback.

"We're down seven points with 50 seconds left. There was a lot of doubt," Frost told reporters after the game.

But, Frost passed the Huskers toward the north end zone. He completed three key passes in the

drive and took Nebraska to the Missouri 12-yard line. After two incompletions, Nebraska faced third down with just seven seconds remaining – time for one more play.

Frost called a slant pattern with wide receiver Shevin Wiggins cutting across the middle from the right side, and wide receiver Matt Davison coming across the end zone from the left side.

Frost fired the ball to the well-covered Wiggins at the goal line. Tiger defensive back Julian Jones slapped the ball away from Wiggins. Safety Harold Piersey reached out his hands to grab the ball. Just then, Wiggins, looking like a soccer player with a bicycle-kick from his back, kicked the ball into the air to keep it alive. Davison darted in from the left side and caught the ball before it touched the ground – or so the officials ruled.

Missouri linebacker Al Sterling: "It wasn't a touchdown, I'm sorry to say. I'm standing two yards from the ball and our whole team was right there."

Missouri cornerback Wade Perkins: "I thought I saw it hit the ground and come up."

Nebraska receiver Matt Davison, who was credited with the catch, begged to differ.

"There was no doubt in my mind that I caught it. I just wanted to see the call before I got all excited about it because it was real close to the ground," he said.

Missouri fans also thought the ball hit the ground. Thinking the Tigers had won, fans rushed the field to tear down the goalposts when the officials signaled touchdown. The scoreboard read: Missouri 38, Nebraska 37 with no time left on the clock. It took a few minutes for the officials to clear the field. When they did, the Huskers kicked the game-tying extra point and forced overtime.

The Missouri crowd was stunned. Elation turned to disbelief. It was the fifth down all over again. How could this happen? How could one school, one team, have so much bad luck – and in the same end zone, the north end zone at Faurot Field? How could one football program lay claim to two of the most bizarre plays in college football, and be on the wrong side of both of them? Those were the questions racing through the minds, hearts, and guts of Tiger fans everywhere.

Overtime went quickly. Nebraska scored on its third play – a 12-yard touchdown run by Frost, his fourth touchdown of the game. Missouri failed to move the ball on its possession. Grant Wistrom and Mike Rucker sacked Jones on fourth down. Game over. Nebraska 45, Missouri 38 OT.

After the game the exhausted coaches met at midfield. Osborne, trying to sense what Larry Smith must have been feeling after an excruciating loss, struggled for words and said, "Great game. Good Luck."

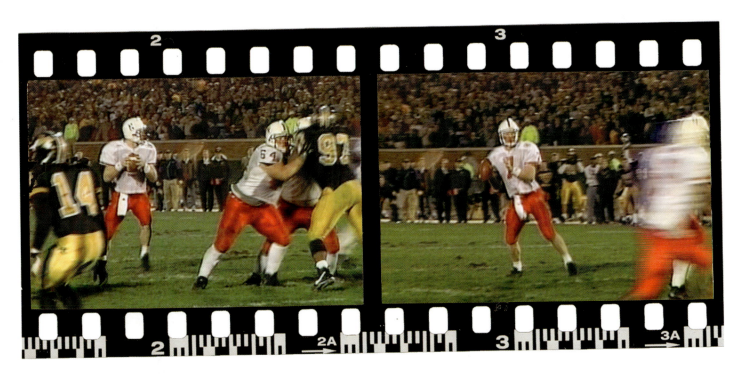

(Opposite) Tiger quarterback Corby Jones kept the Tigers in front until the final play of regulation.

(Above) The beginning of the Flea-Kicker: Husker QB Scott Frost throws to Shevin Wiggins...

Reporters asked Smith what the two coaches said to each other after the game. Smith said Osborne told him the Huskers "got lucky."

"He's right, they did," Smith shot back at reporters.

Was this a moral victory for Missouri? After all, they had the No. 1 team in the nation beaten until the final second, only to lose in overtime.

"There's no satisfaction on the Missouri side," Tiger cornerback Shad Criss told reporters.

Mizzou fullback Ron Janes: "I'm just totally disappointed right now. When I watch it on film I think it's just going to make me sick."

However, following the game, a strange thing happened concerning the polls. Nebraska won, but dropped from first to third in the *Associated Press* Poll. Missouri lost, but moved up to No. 25 in the *AP* Poll, marking the first time the Tigers had been ranked since 1983. The pollsters were certainly impressed with Missouri's showing against the Huskers.

Nebraska finished the season with another national championship, as Tom Osborne retired at season's end. The Tigers finished the regular season 7-4 and went to their first bowl game since 1983, the Holiday Bowl where they lost to Colorado State.

Still, the game will be remembered for one incredible play – the Davison touchdown catch on the final play of the fourth quarter. In Nebraska, Husker fans refer to it as "The Missouri Miracle." On an Internet poll in 1999, Davison's catch was voted by Nebraska fans as the second-greatest play in Husker football history, just behind Johnny Rodgers electrifying punt return against Oklahoma in 1971.

In Missouri the play is known as the "flea-kicker." Tiger fans believe the ball hit the ground. Tiger fans believe Davison didn't make the catch. Tiger fans think Wiggins intentionally kicked the ball in the air and should have been called for a penalty. Tiger fans are still stunned by the final seconds of the fourth quarter in the 1997 Nebraska game.

"One stinkin' play."

...(Left to right) The Flea-Kicker continued: (top three) Mizzou's Julian Jones and Harold Piersey go for the ball. (middle three) Wiggins kicks the ball to a diving Matt Davison. (bottom three) Touchdown, Nebraska (Courtesy Mizzou Sports Properties/KOMU).

The scoreboard says it all!

Missouri 41   Nebraska 24

Vindicated and Victorious
OCTOBER 11, 2003

Twenty-five years is a long time.

When a married couple makes it to its 25th wedding anniversary, it's a big deal – the silver anniversary. Twenty-five years after graduating from high school or college is a major reunion. Twenty-five years at the same job is a major milestone. A 25-year professional sports career for an athlete is almost unheard of.

One team beating another team in any sport for 25 years is called dominating for the winner and embarrassing for the loser. And that's how Missouri football fans felt toward Nebraska when the Tigers squared off against the Cornhuskers for their game at Faurot Field in 2003. The last time Missouri beat Nebraska in a football game was in 1978. Twenty-five years of losing to the same team. Some close calls. Some blowouts. All losses. Twenty-five years. A quarter of a century. That's a long time.

In 2003, Nebraska once again came to Faurot Field with a strong team. The Cornhuskers, ranked tenth in the nation, were undefeated and boasted the top-ranked defense in college football.

The Tigers also had some early season success. They were 4-1, but coming off an embarrassing 35-14 loss to Kansas. Now, add in the fact that the Tigers had not beaten a Top 10 ranked team since 1981. Streaks have to end sometime, and the sellout crowd of 68,349 fans, on a cool drizzly night at Faurot Field, sensed something was about to give.

The Cornhuskers temporarily dampened the home crowd spirits. They scored first when quarterback Jamaal Lord hit Mark LeFlore on a

Mizzou fans from the stadium begin to fill the field shortly after the game ends.

Memorable Moments • 133

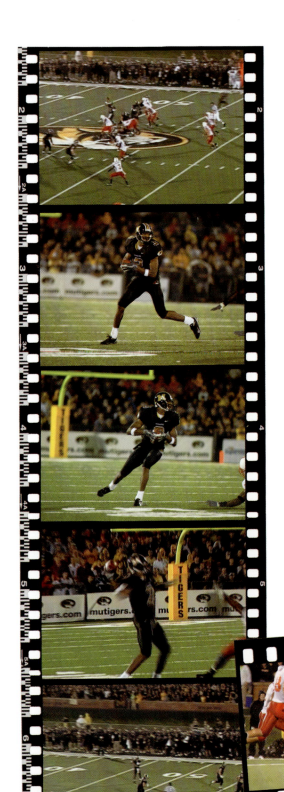

(Top to bottom, left to right) Tiger quarterback Brad Smith passes to former Tiger quarterback Darius Outlaw - now a receiver - who passes back to Smith across the field. Smith sprints down the sideline, hurdles his own blocker around the 20-yard line and outraces the Cornhuskers to complete the 47-yard touchdown play (Courtesy Mizzou Sports Properties/KOMU).

screen pass. LeFlore raced 55 yards through the Tiger defense for a touchdown and a 7-0 Nebraska lead.

Missouri responded. With the rain coming down and the ball getting slick, the Tigers' Brock Harvey punted the ball to the 4-yard line. Nebraska return man Josh Davis fumbled the wet ball and the Tigers recovered at the Nebraska 6-yard line. Two plays later, Zack Abron rammed his way across the goal line to tie the game 7-7.

Early in the second quarter the Tigers took the lead with a little trickery and the athletic ability of their current quarterback, and their former quarterback. With the ball on the Nebraska 47-yard line, Mizzou quarterback Brad Smith called a "Diamond Throwback Screen" and handed the ball off to receiver Darius Outlaw on an end-around to the right side. Outlaw, the former quarterback, stopped and threw the ball back across the field to Smith, who had an ample escort of blockers and sprinted down the sideline for a touchdown. It was Smith's first career touchdown catch.

The razzle-dazzle electrified the crowd and gave the Tigers a 14-7 lead. Sometimes to break a 25-year losing streak you have to resort to a little trickery. The play foreshadowed events to come, as the Tigers would throw caution to the wind.

Nebraska added a field goal just before the end of the first half and trailed the Tigers 14-10. At halftime, Mizzou honored former coach Warren Powers and his players. It was a fitting tribute. After all, Powers was the last Mizzou coach, and his players were the last Tigers to beat Nebraska back in 1978.

Despite a four-point lead and 30 minutes to play, Missouri did not come out of the locker room on fire. In fact, the Tigers were somewhat flat.

The third quarter belonged to the Cornhuskers who scored two touchdowns. Running back David Horne scored on a 5-yard run midway in the period and Jamaal Lord scored on a 35-yard run near the end of the third quarter to give the Huskers a 24-14 lead. Momentum was on the Huskers side. They had a 10-point lead with 15 minutes to play.

Could the Tigers regain momentum and close the 10-point lead in only one quarter? Or would Nebraska, with the No. 1 ranked defense in the nation, extend its winning streak to 25 in a row over the Tigers? Missouri answered those questions quickly and decisively in perhaps the most memorable quarter of football ever at Faurot Field.

On the first play in the fourth quarter, on third-and-four, Brad Smith called his own number and scored on a 39-yard run to the end zone. Mizzou pulled it within three points and trailed 24-21.

The Tigers struck quickly again. After recovering a Husker fumble at the Nebraska 9-yard line, the Tigers offense stalled. Mizzou lined up for a game-tying 32-yard field goal attempt. Now, more trickery and more gambling. The Tigers faked the field goal. Holder and back-up quarterback Sonny Riccio took the snap and ran to the right side. He lofted a pass to tight end Victor Sesay in the right corner of the end zone. Touchdown Missouri! The Tigers took the lead 28-24 with 11:21 left in the fourth quarter.

"We were pretty confident. We worked on it (the fake field goal) all last week and this week," Riccio told reporters after the game.

So when did he know it was going to be good?

(Top to bottom, left to right) Tiger backup QB Sonny Riccio, off a fake field goal, passes to Victor Sesay for the go-ahead touchdown (Courtesy Mizzou Sports Properties/KOMU).

Memorable Moments • 135

"I knew as soon as it left my hand," Riccio added.

The gamble paid off. Instead of a tie game, Mizzou had a four-point lead. Still, 11 minutes left in the game. Tiger fans weren't celebrating – they were holding their breath. They'd seen fourth quarter leads turn south before. But, that wouldn't happen in this game.

Nebraska got the ball back, but the Tiger defense stopped the Huskers – three-and-out. After the Husker punt and a Marcus James return, the Tigers had the ball at the Husker 36-yard line. Eight plays later, Smith scored on a short run around right end, and the Tigers led 34-24. Six minutes to play, but still, Tiger fans held their breath. The celebration though, would soon begin.

The Tigers became a runaway freight train heading downhill, and the Huskers were in their way. When Nebraska got the ball back, Tiger defensive end Zach Ville intercepted Lord and ran the ball to the Husker 7-yard line. Two plays later, Smith scored his fourth touchdown of the game on a 9-yard quarterback draw. Missouri 41, Nebraska 24.

Now the celebration began, and it lasted the final five minutes of the game. And it lasted after the game with thousands of fans storming the field and tearing down the goalposts. Most of the crowd stayed in their seats. They didn't leave the stadium. They wanted to soak in the moment. Marching Mizzou played on. The Tiger faithful sang the fight song and clapped to the "Missouri Waltz." The celebration lasted through the night and into the morning. It was a celebration Tiger fans had waited 25 years for.

Mizzou linebacker James Kinney summed it up, telling reporters after the game, "This was a win for all the fans that have been waiting for this for 20-something years. And it's for all the players that played before us."

The victory was so decisive. Nebraska's defense had given up only 38 points in its first five games. Mizzou scored 41 points in one game and 27 points in the fourth quarter. The Tigers gained 452 yards in total offense against the top ranked defense in the nation, and Smith had 350 yards in total offense and tied a school record with four touchdowns.

"I told my wife the other night I'm tired of watching people upsetting other people," head coach Gary Pinkel told the media after the game.

The Tigers and Pinkel certainly had a different attitude leading up to the Nebraska game. In their first five games, including their loss to Kansas, the Tigers looked tentative, almost afraid to make mistakes. In practices leading up to Nebraska, Pinkel ordered his players to be more aggressive, to not worry so much about mistakes, and to just make plays.

"Our whole goal was just to play loose and try to make plays. We were just wide open and it felt really good. It was fun," quarterback Brad Smith understatedly told the media after the game.

"I've been waiting for a win like this for five years," chimed in Darius Outlaw.

Five years – oh to be young. Older Mizzou fans had waited 25 years for a win like this. The Tiger victory over Nebraska in 2003 may not have been the greatest win in Missouri football history, but because of the 25-year losing streak to the Huskers, it certainly was the sweetest for Tiger football fans everywhere.

Twenty-five years is a long time.

(Opposite and above)
Let the celebration begin.

Afterword
By John Kadlec

Memories of Mizzou football? I probably sound like fellow Missouri native – Yogi Berra – when I say, "I have more Missouri memories than I can remember."

Missouri means everything to me. I've spent the better part of my adult life associated with Mizzou football in one form or another. To me, it's a great, great tradition.

I still get a knot in my stomach before every game. Sitting in the broadcast booth I'm still thinking, "We gotta win this game."

And, when I get ready to go, I turn to Mike Kelly and say, "Kelly, we gotta kick the hell out of 'em today!"

My Missouri memories start when I came to school here in 1948. I was green as grass and scared of the coaches. But, I was fortunate to play for the legendary Don Faurot.

Don and his assistants – especially "Hi" Simmons – were really fantastic to the young kids. And, after my senior season, I received my greatest honor in football – when Coach Faurot selected me to his All-Offensive and All-Defensive teams. I made All-Conference but that didn't mean anything compared to what Coach Faurot did for me.

When all is said and done, that's what I remember most about Tiger football – the people.

Sure, we played in many remarkable games, including the unforgettable moments highlighted in this book. But, I'll always remember the wonderful people who I've

"Mr. Mizzou," John Kadlec, shown on the sidelines during the Tigers' upset of Nebraska in 1973

had the privilege to work with over the years – the Tiger coaches, players and fans who created those lasting memories.

Great fans, incredibly loyal fans.

Great players, great kids.

Great coaches. Head coaches like Don Faurot, Frank Broyles, Dan Devine and Al Onofrio. And, fellow assistants – Clay Cooper, Harry Smith and Rollie Dotsch, just to name a few.

Don Faurot probably knew more about football, offensively and defensively, than any football coach I've ever known. He was an outstanding football coach in every way.

Dan Devine was a great recruiter and great motivator, the greatest motivator I've ever seen in college coaching. And, he listened to his coaches. I really enjoyed coaching for him.

Still, I can't forget the games – the upsets, the nail-biters, even the heartbreakers.

Kansas State, 1969. Now, that was a tremendous football game. We should've charged double admission to that one. To this day, I talk to K-Staters and they say that's the greatest game they've ever seen – and they lost, 41-38.

That was my No. 1 game until 2003. When we beat Nebraska – for the first time in 25 years – I had tears in my eyes. If you're a Missouri fan and didn't have tears in your eyes, you're nuts. It was a terrific game and our kids deserved it.

But, as much I enjoy look back at all the magnificent memories, I'm extremely excited about the future of Tiger football.

I've never seen a coach so aware and so organized as Gary Pinkel. Give Gary Pinkel some time and he'll exceed Dan Devine's victory total.

Dan was a great organizer but this guy is better. The organization of his staff, his work on and off the football field, and his awareness of his kids – those are the reasons for Gary Pinkel's success so far.

So, here's to the future of Tiger football! But let's never forget our glorious past.

John Kadlec

John Kadlec

Longtime Mizzou ambassador John Kadlec ("Mr. Mizzou" to many Tiger fans) played and coached for Don Faurot and coached for Frank Broyles, Dan Devine and Al Onofrio. He is the color analyst for the Tiger Network. He was inducted into the Missouri Hall of Fame in 1996.

Acknowledgements

As part of our licensing agreement with the University of Missouri we were granted permission and authorized to use pictures, graphics, and logos from the university and its various publications and archives. We have made efforts to attribute materials used in this book that were not part of that licensing agreement. If any errors have been made, we will be happy to correct them in future editions.

In addition, this book would not have been possible without the tremendous cooperation and assistance from a number of extremely talented and devoted individuals and the organizations which they represent:

The Athletic Department of the University of Missouri with special thanks to Athletic Director Mike Alden, Senior Associate Athletic Director Mario Moccia, Chad Moller and his media relations staff, Marketing Director Frank Cuervo, and Director of Community Relations Mike Kelly.

Missouri Head Coach Gary Pinkel and "Mr. Mizzou" John Kadlec, who graciously consented to write the foreword and afterword.

The Archives of the University of Missouri with special thanks to reference archivist Gary Cox and Michael Holland.

Laird Veatch and Mizzou Sports Properties/Learfield Communications

Linda Gilbert, University of Missouri trademark and licensing program administrator.

Todd McCubbin and David Roloff and the University of Missouri Alumni Association

Becky Diehl, *Savitar* and *Maneater*

Dale Smith and Rob Hill of Publications and Alumni Communications

Neff Productions and its "100 Years of Missouri Football."

State Historical Society of Missouri

KOMU-TV with special thanks to Ben Arnett, Garrett Gordon, Chris Gervino and Jim Riek

Tom Warhover and the *Columbia Missourian*

Fox Sports Net archives

University of Nebraska and Husker Vision Archives

Pacific Life Holiday Bowl with special thanks to Mark Neville and Nathan Wauthier

University of Southern California, in particular Tim Tessalone

The Ohio State University

Harry Smith

To our many friends and fellow alums – with whom we built lasting relationships at the University of Missouri – who provided us with advice, support and encouragement during the planning, writing and production of this book especially Warren Mills, Jim Scilligo, Tim Cochran, Cynthia Schreen and Mike Beck.

Jeff, Scott, Kevin and Paula Gerber Donoho

Jim and Patricia O'Brien

Special appreciation to Steve Mull, Travis Gallup and Scott Rule of The Donning Company Publishers, a subsidiary of Walsworth Publishing Company, for their guidance, marketing assistance and superb design of this book.

Our sincere thanks to all the sportswriters and photographers – many of whom are Mizzou graduates – who chronicled Tiger football throughout the years.

Most of all, our undying gratitude goes to the players and coaches who created those wonderful and memorable moments in Tiger football history. And, of course, we extend our sincere thanks to the loyal fans of Missouri football, who will never let these memories die.

About the Authors

Todd Donoho and Dan O'Brien graduated from the University of Missouri in 1977 with Bachelor of Journalism degrees. They met during their freshman year and have been friends ever since.

Donoho is an award-winning television and radio sportscaster having worked in Grand Rapids, Michigan; Cincinnati, Ohio; and Los Angeles, California. He appeared in the movie "Blue Chips" and hosted the nationally televised sports program "Time Out For Trivia."

Donoho currently resides in Columbia, Missouri.

O'Brien is also an award-winning sportscaster having worked in Miami, Florida; Washington D.C.; Pittsburgh, Pennsylvania; and Indianapolis, Indiana. He has written a screenplay about flamboyant Baseball Hall of Famer Rube Waddell.

O'Brien currently resides in the Indianapolis area.

The picture you see here was taken more than a few years ago and is a memorable moment they choose to preserve.